THINK THAI

A Mindset Shift for Fluency

Stop Translating,
Start Thinking Like a Native

BY ADRIAN GEE

ISBN: 979-8-292722-30-4

AUTHOR'S NOTE

Hey friend,

Thanks for picking this up. Whether you grabbed this book out of curiosity, motivation, or pure obsession with learning Thai—I'm glad you're here. Seriously. Writing this book has been a passion project rooted in my obsession with mastering languages and pushing the boundaries of how fast someone can actually *think* in another language.

This isn't your typical Thai textbook. There are no dusty grammar charts, no forced exercises, and zero fluff. Just practical, punchy, real-world tools designed to rewire your brain into a Thai-speaking machine—without ever translating in your head.

And here's the thing: I'm not a traditional language teacher. I'm a creator, a communicator, and someone who believes that the faster you can *think* like a native speaker, the faster you can live a fuller, richer life across borders and cultures.

That's why I've also prepared a little bonus for you—a free gift waiting at **www.seebbly.com**. It's designed to keep you on track, motivated, and connected with a global tribe of learners who are on the same mission.

If you want to reach out, connect, or share your progress, come find me on Instagram: **@adriangruszka.** I'd love to hear your story.

Here's to thinking in Thai, speaking with confidence, and living life on your terms.

Let's make it happen.

- *Adrian Gee*

CONTENTS

INTRODUCTION

WHY THIS BOOK EXISTS

Let's cut the fluff.

This isn't a book about grammar rules, verb charts, or perfect Thai.

It's a book about rewiring your brain.

About finally reaching that moment where you stop *translating*… and start *thinking* in Thai.

You know the one. Where you hear someone say something in Thai, and instead of breaking it down like a puzzle, you just *get it*. Instantly. Instinctively. Like it's your own thought.

I wrote this book because I know what it's like to feel stuck. To be months—even years—into learning Thai and still feel like a fraud every time you try to speak. To have all the words in your head, but none on your tongue when it actually matters.

I know what it's like to freeze mid-sentence because your brain's still negotiating with English. To feel like your mouth is constantly two seconds behind the conversation.

This book is my answer to that.

Because here's the truth:

You don't become fluent by memorizing more.
You become fluent by letting go.

By rewiring the way you think. The way you process. The way you speak.

That's what *Think in Thai* is about.

Not about passing a test.
Not about sounding perfect.
Not about impressing anyone.

It's about unlocking a mindset that lets you speak Thai without fear, without hesitation, and without needing English as your crutch.

Inside this book, you'll find personal stories—some hilarious, some painful, all real. You'll find practical drills that actually train your brain. And you'll find a philosophy of language learning that's focused on *freedom*, not perfection.

Whether you're trying to flirt in Thai, land a job, connect with locals while traveling, or just stop sounding like Google Translate, you're in the right place.

This book is a little weird. A little raw. A little different.

But if you're still reading, maybe so are you.

Let's make Thai a part of your life—not just something you study, but something you *live.*

Let's get started!

CHAPTER ONE:
How the Brain Learns a Language

THE TAXI DRIVER WHO EXPOSED MY BIGGEST WEAKNESS

I still remember the exact moment I realized my Thai was useless.

It wasn't when I struggled through a YouTube lesson.
It wasn't when I mispronounced a word in a restaurant.
It was inside a battered, white taxi speeding through the streets of Bangkok.

I had just arrived in Thailand, exhausted but excited. I'd spent months preparing for this trip—hours buried in Thai textbooks, drilling flashcards, memorizing tones and sentence patterns until I could recite them in my sleep. I felt **ready.**

So when I slid into the backseat of the cab and the driver turned around with a friendly smile, I was confident.

- "ไปไหนครับ บอส?"

I froze.

I knew บอส meant "boss"—like "man" or "dude," friendly and casual. I knew ไปไหน meant "go where."
I even vaguely recognized ครับ as a polite particle.

But somehow, my brain **couldn't put it together.**

I sat there, staring at him, my mind desperately running through every Thai word I'd ever learned, trying to **translate his sentence word-for-word in my head** like a puzzle I had to solve. The problem was, by the time I worked out that he was simply asking, *"Where are we going?"* he was already looking at me like I might need medical attention.

I panicked and blurted out in English: *"Uh… the city center?"*

He sighed, shook his head, and started driving.

I spent the rest of the ride **furious with myself.**

How could this be happening? I had **studied Thai for months**—I had memorized hundreds of words, taken online courses, watched Thai Netflix shows with subtitles. And yet, when faced with **a real conversation**, my brain had completely shut down.

It felt like all my knowledge was trapped inside a glass box—I could see it, but I couldn't **use** it.

That's when it hit me.

I had been learning Thai **the wrong way.**

I was treating it like **a math equation,** trying to translate every word before I could understand the meaning. **But that's not how language works.**

Native speakers don't **pause and translate in their heads**—they process language **naturally, in real-time.**

And if I ever wanted to **truly** speak Thai, I had to train my brain to do the same.

Why Your Brain Struggles to Learn Thai Like a Native Speaker

Have you ever felt like you *know* Thai but **can't actually speak it?** Do you recognize words when you see them written, but freeze up when you need to **say something out loud?**

That's because your brain is still in **translation mode.**

When you learn Thai the **traditional way** (memorizing vocabulary lists, drilling grammar rules, translating sentences word-for-word), you're using a completely **different mental process** than a native speaker.

And that's exactly why fluency feels **so far away.**

HOW THE BRAIN STORES AND RETRIEVES THAI

Imagine this: You walk into a café in Thailand, and the waiter asks, "รับอะไรดีครับ?"

If you've heard this phrase many times before, your brain **immediately** recognizes it as, *"What would you like to have?"* You don't break it down word by word. You don't translate it into English. **You just understand it.**

But if you're still learning Thai, your brain **doesn't retrieve the phrase instantly.** Instead, it goes through a slow, clunky process:

1. **Recognize** individual words (รับ = receive/order, อะไร = what, ดี = good).
2. **Try to recall** how the words fit together.
3. **Mentally translate** the sentence into English.
4. **Construct a response in English, then translate it back into Thai.**
5. **Finally say something… if you haven't already frozen.**

This is why so many learners **struggle to speak quickly**—their brain hasn't built **automatic recall pathways** yet.

The good news? You can **train your brain** to retrieve Thai words as fast as a native speaker. But to do that, you need to understand **how memory works** when learning a language.

How Your Brain Stores and Retrieves Words in Thai

Your brain has two major types of memory that determine how well you retain Thai:

1. Short-Term Memory (The 'Temporary Storage')

- Think of short-term memory as **a notepad**—it holds information for a few seconds or minutes before erasing it.
- When you hear a new Thai word, it enters **short-term memory first.**
- If you don't **use or review it,** your brain **forgets it within minutes.**

Example: You hear the word "เก้าอี้" (chair) for the first time. You repeat it once, but by the next day, you've completely forgotten it. **Why?** Because it never made it to long-term memory.

2. Long-Term Memory (The 'Permanent Storage')

- Long-term memory is like **a hard drive**—it stores information for **days, months, or even a lifetime.**
- For a Thai word to move from **short-term to long-term memory,** your brain needs **multiple exposures and uses.**
- The more you **retrieve** a word (through speaking, writing, or listening), the stronger the memory becomes.

Example: If you hear the word "เก้าอี้" in a conversation, read it in a book, see it on a sign, and use it in a sentence, your brain will **automatically store it for future use.**

Tip: The goal of fluency is to move as many Thai words as possible from short-term to long-term memory—so that recalling them becomes instant.

Why Some Thai Words Stick & Others Disappear

Have you ever noticed that certain Thai words **stick in your brain immediately,** while others **seem impossible to remember?**

That's because words move into long-term memory only when they are connected to strong mental triggers.

Words You Remember Instantly:

- Words tied to **emotions** (e.g., you'll never forget **ร้อน** means "hot" after telling someone **ฉันร้อน** when you meant "I'm horny").
- Words you **use frequently** (e.g., greetings like "สวัสดี" and "ขอบคุณ").
- Words with **strong mental images** (e.g., the first time you see a giant จิ้งจก climbing your hotel wall in Chiang Mai, you'll never forget the word for gecko!).

Words You Keep Forgetting:

- Words you **only see once in a textbook** but never hear or use in conversation.
- Words with **no personal connection** (e.g., obscure vocabulary like "สายล่อฟ้า" (lightning rod) that has no relevance to your life).
- Words that **aren't tied to real-world experiences** (e.g., memorizing verb patterns without ever hearing them used naturally).

Takeaway: If you want to make Thai words **stick forever,** you need to **connect them to real experiences, emotions, and frequent usage.**

The Three Key Methods to Retain Thai Forever

1. Repetition: Exposing Your Brain to the Same Words Again & Again

- Your brain **remembers what it sees most often.**
- The more times you **see, hear, and say** a Thai word, the deeper it is stored in long-term memory.

Example Strategy:

- Write new words on sticky notes and place them around your house.
- Use **spaced repetition apps** like Anki or Quizlet to review vocabulary daily.
- Say new words out loud **multiple times a day** to reinforce them.

2. Immersion: Surrounding Yourself with Thai

- **Passive immersion** (hearing Thai without consciously studying) trains your brain to **recognize words effortlessly.**
- Even if you don't understand everything, **your brain absorbs patterns** and starts retrieving words faster.

Example Strategy:

- Change your **phone & social media settings** to Thai.
- Listen to **Thai podcasts or YouTube videos daily.**
- Watch Netflix in Thai **without subtitles** (or with Thai subtitles only).

3. Active Recall: Training Your Brain to Retrieve Words Quickly

- **Most learners passively recognize words but struggle to recall them in real-time.**
- To train fluency, you need to **force your brain to recall words without hints.**

Example Strategy:

- Cover the Thai side of your flashcards and try recalling the word from memory.
- Try **describing objects around you in Thai** without looking up words.
- **Speak out loud every day,** even if you're talking to yourself.

Reflection Exercise: How Do You Store Thai in Your Brain?

Answer the following questions to analyze your memory habits:

1. Think of 5 Thai words you learned recently. Do you still remember them? If not, why do you think they disappeared from your memory?
2. What Thai words have stuck in your brain effortlessly? What made them memorable?
3. Are you relying more on passive recognition (understanding words when you see them) or active recall (retrieving words on demand)? How can you improve this?

WHY BABIES LEARN NATURALLY (AND WHAT WE CAN COPY)

The 3-Year-Old Who Spoke Better Thai Than Me

I was sitting in a park in Chiang Mai, sipping my coffee, when I overheard a little boy—maybe **three years old**—chattering away with his mother.

"แม่ หนูอยากไปเล่นชิงช้า"
("Mom, I want to go to the swings.")

"กินน้ำส้มให้หมดก่อนลูก"
("First, finish your orange juice.")

"หนูกินหมดแล้ว ไปกันเถอะ ไปๆๆ!"
("But I already finished! Let's go, let's go, let's go!")

I watched, half in awe, half in frustration. This **tiny human** had been alive for barely three years, and yet he was **effortlessly communicating in Thai**—no hesitation, no mistakes, no mental translation.

Meanwhile, here I was, an adult who had spent **months** studying Thai, and I was still struggling to form basic sentences without stopping to think.

It made me wonder: **What do babies do differently?**

The answer? **They absorb language in a completely different way than adults.**

Why Do Babies Learn Languages So Easily?

It's a common myth that children are **naturally better** at learning languages. The truth is, **they aren't "better"—they just learn differently.**

Here's what's happening inside a baby's brain:

1. Babies Learn Through Immersion (Not Studying)

- Babies **hear** their language **24/7**—from parents, cartoons, songs, and people around them.
- They don't sit down with textbooks or memorize grammar rules—they simply **absorb Thai naturally.**
- Their brains **constantly connect words to real-life experiences** (e.g., hearing "น้ำ" while drinking water).

Contrast with Adults: Most adults study Thai for **30 minutes a day at most,** then switch back to English. The brain doesn't get enough **Thai input** to form deep connections.

2. Babies Are Fearless (They Don't Care About Mistakes)

- A baby doesn't think, *"What if I say this wrong?"*—they just speak.
- They make **tons of mistakes,** but **no one corrects them aggressively**—they learn by trial and error.

Contrast with Adults: Many adult learners **fear sounding stupid** when speaking Thai, so they hesitate, overthink, and avoid speaking at all.

3. Babies Learn by Repetition, Not Translation

- A baby hears "เอาลูกบอลให้แม่หน่อย" (Give the ball to Mom) **hundreds of times** before they understand it.
- They **never** think: "เอา = *give,* ลูกบอล = *ball,* ให้ = *to give,* แม่ = *mom.*" They just **understand it as a whole phrase.**

Contrast with Adults: Adults often **try to translate everything in their heads,** which slows them down.

What Adults Have That Babies Don't (And How It Gives Us an Advantage)

Here's the **good news:** Adults can actually learn languages **faster than babies**—if we use the right techniques.

1. Adults Can Learn Consciously

- Babies learn **by accident**—they pick up language because they're constantly exposed to it.
- Adults can **learn on purpose**—we can **speed up the process** by deliberately practicing, setting goals, and actively improving.

2. Adults Recognize Patterns Faster

- A baby needs to hear a sentence **hundreds of times** before they understand a grammar rule.
- An adult can **see the pattern instantly** and start applying it right away.

Example:

- A baby needs to hear a sentence hundreds of times before they understand a grammar rule.
- An adult can **learn this in 5 minutes** and apply it immediately.

3. Adults Can Learn Multiple Ways

- Babies **only** learn through hearing and repetition.
- Adults can **combine** listening, reading, writing, speaking, and grammar study for maximum speed.

The secret to learning Thai fast?

Use **the strengths of adults (conscious learning, pattern recognition, and multi-method exposure)** while copying the **natural** way babies absorb language.

3 Strategies to Mimic Baby-Like Learning (But Faster!)

1. The "Drown Your Brain in Thai" Method

What Babies Do: Hear Thai **all day, every day.**
How You Copy It: Surround yourself with Thai as much as possible.

Example:

- Change your **phone & apps to Thai**
- Listen to **Thai music & podcasts daily**
- Watch Netflix in **Thai without subtitles**
- Read simple **Thai books & articles**

2. The "Speak Like a Child" Challenge

What Babies Do: Speak without fear—even if they make mistakes.
How You Copy It: Force yourself to **speak Thai daily,** no matter how bad it sounds.

Example:

- **Talk to yourself** in Thai every morning
- **Narrate your daily activities** in Thai
- **Speak with a native tutor and accept mistakes as part of learning**

Rule: No overthinking. No translation. Just say something.

3. The "No Translation Game"

What Babies Do: Learn words **without translating** into another language.
How You Copy It: Train your brain to **think in Thai** instead of translating.

Example:

- **Look at objects around you** and name them in Thai (never in English).
- **Picture** words in your head instead of thinking of the English translation.
- **Use Thai definitions** instead of English ones.

  Example: Instead of learning:

  - หมา = Dog

  Learn:

  - หมา = สัตว์ที่เห่าและเป็นเพื่อนที่ดีที่สุดของมนุษย์ (An animal that barks and is man's best friend.)

Fun Exercise: Absorb Thai Like a Baby

Your Mission: Go Full Baby Mode for 24 Hours!

For **one entire day,** do **everything** in Thai:

- ✓ **Think in Thai.** (No English allowed in your thoughts.)
- ✓ **Listen to Thai all day.** (Podcasts, music, or Netflix in Thai.)
- ✓ **Only speak in Thai.** (If you can't form a sentence, just use the words you know.)

Goal: At the end of the day, notice how much **easier** it is to recall words & respond naturally!

Now that you understand how your brain stores and retrieves Thai, it's time to tackle the **biggest reason learners struggle to speak fluently—mental translation.**

The reason I froze in that Bangkok taxi wasn't because I didn't know the words. It was because my brain was **stuck translating instead of thinking in Thai.** Instead of recognizing the phrase "ไปไหนครับ บอส?" instantly, I was **mentally breaking it down piece by piece,** trying to solve it like a math problem.

This slow, word-for-word process is what holds most learners back. If you've ever struggled to form sentences quickly or felt like you knew Thai but couldn't speak it in real conversations, it's because your brain hasn't yet made the switch to **processing Thai directly.**

But don't worry—this is something you can **train.**

In the next chapter, we'll break down exactly **why translation slows you down, how native speakers process language differently, and how you can rewire your brain to think in Thai naturally.**

You're about to take a major step toward fluency—let's go.

CHAPTER TWO:
Breaking the Translation Habit

THE DAY I EMBARRASSED MYSELF IN A THAI BAR

Bangkok. A warm summer night. The air was thick with the smell of sizzling garlic, grilled pork skewers, and the sharp herbal kick of nam prik dipping sauce. I had been in Thailand for a few weeks now, and I was **feeling good about my Thai**—maybe even a little too good.

After all, at this point I had already spent **months** learning the language. I had drilled vocabulary flashcards, listened to Thai podcasts, and even practiced tones out loud like a crazy person. My confidence was high.

That night, I walked into a lively bar near Sukhumvit, packed with locals. A group of uncles leaned against the counter, drinking small Chang beers and debating something that clearly involved a lot of exaggerated facial expressions and clapping. A couple whispered to each other over a shared plate of grilled squid. The bartender, a rugged guy in his fifties with a gold chain and a tattoo peeking out of his sleeve, wiped down the bar and gave me a quick nod.

I took a deep breath. *This was my moment to shine.*

I walked up to the bar, placed my hands confidently on the smooth wood, and locked eyes with the bartender.

- "จะดื่มอะไรดีครับ?" (What would you like to drink?) he asked.

And this… this is where things went horribly wrong.

Lost in Translation: The Fatal Mistake

I meant to say *"I'm hot"*—because, well, it was a humid summer night, and I was sweating through my t-shirt.

So, without hesitation, I proudly responded:

- "ผมร้อนแรง!"

For a second, silence. The bartender froze mid-wipe. The couple next to me stopped whispering. One of the old men at the counter **choked on his beer.** Then—**laughter.** A full-blown explosion of laughter that echoed through the bar.

I stood there, confused. Had I said it wrong? Was my tone off? What was so funny?

The bartender leaned in, barely able to contain his grin.

- "พี่ว่าเราไม่ได้ตั้งใจจะพูดแบบนั้นนะครับ"
("I don't think you meant to say that.")

I stared back at him, my confidence draining like a leaky faucet.

- "ทำไมล่ะครับ?" (Why?)

One of the old men at the counter turned to me, still wheezing from laughing so hard.

- "เพราะ 'ร้อนแรง' ไม่ได้แปลว่า 'I'm hot' แบบอากาศร้อน... มันแปลว่า 'I'm sexy.'"

A Lesson I'll Never Forget

I felt the blood rush to my face faster than I could say "ขอโทษครับ." My brain scrambled for a way to recover. What I *should* have said was:

- "ผมรู้สึกร้อน" (Literally: *I feel hot*—the correct way to say *I'm feeling warm* in Thai.)

Instead, I had just confidently announced to a packed Bangkok bar that **I was feeling irresistibly sexy.**

Fantastic.

For the rest of the night, I tried to blend into my barstool as much as possible. The bartender—after wiping away a few tears of laughter—gave me a free drink, probably as a reward for providing the best entertainment of the evening.

But as embarrassing as it was, **that moment taught me something I would never forget.**

Up until that night, I had been **translating everything in my head.** I was still thinking in English, just **converting** it into Thai word-for-word. But languages don't work like that.

Some phrases **just don't translate directly**—and sometimes, getting it wrong means making a complete fool of yourself.

That was the day I realized that **word-for-word translation is a trap.**

It slows you down. It makes you sound unnatural. And, in the worst cases, it leads to **disaster-level mistakes** like mine.

If you want to think and speak in Thai **fluently,** you have to **break free from the translation habit** and start **processing Thai as its own language**—without filtering it through English first.

In this chapter, we're going to break down:

- **Why translating in your head is holding you back**
- **The structural differences between Thai and English that make direct translation impossible**
- **How to train your brain to think in Thai instinctively**

Trust me—by the end of this chapter, you won't just avoid embarrassing mistakes like mine… you'll be able to **respond in Thai naturally, without pausing to translate.**

Let's get started.

THE TRAP OF WORD-FOR-WORD TRANSLATION

Why Thinking in English is Sabotaging Your Thai

You walk into a café in Chiang Mai. The waiter greets you with a friendly:

- “รับอะไรดีคะ?” (*What would you like?)*

You confidently reply, translating straight from English:

- “ฉันสามารถมีหนึ่งกาแฟได้ไหม?” (*I can have a coffee.)*

The waiter raises an eyebrow. Something about your sentence sounds… off.

The **correct** way to order in Thai is:

- “ขอกาแฟหนึ่งแก้วค่ะ” (*Can I have one coffee?)*
- “เอากาแฟหนึ่งค่ะ” (*I'll take a coffee.)*
- “อยากได้กาแฟค่ะ” (*I want a coffee.)*

Nobody says **“ฉันสามารถมีกาแฟได้ไหม”** in Thai. That's an English structure, **word-for-word translated into Thai.**

And this is exactly where most Thai learners go wrong.

Why Word-for-Word Translation is a Trap

When you translate **word by word** instead of **thinking in Thai,** you run into three major problems:

1. **Your sentences sound unnatural.**
2. **You say things that don't make sense.**
3. **You hesitate and slow down in conversations.**

This happens because English and Thai **don't have a 1:1 relationship**—many words and phrases don't translate directly.

Real-Life Translation Fails (That Could Happen to You)

Translation mistakes aren't just **awkward**—they can be **downright embarrassing.**

Here are some **real-world** examples of learners getting stuck in the **word-for-word translation trap:**

- ### Translation Fail #1: "I'm Hot" → "ผมร้อนแรง"

  What You Meant: *I'm feeling warm.*
  What You Actually Said: *I'm sexy.*

  Correct Way to Say It in Thai:
  รู้สึกร้อน *(I feel hot.)*

- **Translation Fail #2: "I'm Excited" → "ฉันตื่นเต้นมาก" (with wrong tone)**

  What You Meant: *I'm excited.*
  What You Actually Said: *I'm nervous/scared (depending on intonation).*

  Correct Way to Say It in Thai:
  ดีใจมาก **or** ตื่นเต้นมาก *(with correct tone and context)*

- **Translation Fail #3: "Can You Lend Me a Hand?" → "คุณให้มือฉันหน่อยได้ไหม?"**

  What You Meant: *Can you help me?*
  What You Actually Said: *Can you give me your literal hand?*

  Correct Way to Say It in Thai:
  ช่วยฉันหน่อยได้ไหม? *(Can you help me?)*

- **Translation Fail #4: "I'm Full" → "ฉันเต็มแล้ว"**

  What You Meant: *I've had enough food.*
  What You Actually Said: *I'm full… like a container.*

  Correct Way to Say It in Thai:
  อิ่มแล้ว *(I'm full from eating.)*

- **Translation Fail #5: "I Forgot My Homework" → "ฉันลืมการบ้านของฉัน"**

  What You Meant: *I forgot my homework.*
  What You Actually Said: *Sounds robotic and overly literal.*

  Correct Way to Say It in Thai:
  ลืมเอาการบ้านมา **or** ลืมทำการบ้าน *(I forgot to bring/do my homework.)*

Why Thai and English Don't Translate Directly

Word-for-word translation doesn't work because **Thai structures sentences differently than English.**

English	Wrong Thai Translation	Correct Thai Sentence
I am 25 years old.	ฉันคือ 25 ปีแก่แล้ว	อายุยี่สิบห้าปี (I'm 25 years old.)
It's cold today.	มันหนาววันนี้ (Sounds like "It is cold, today.")	วันนี้อากาศหนาว (Today the weather is cold.)
I like coffee.	ฉันชอบกาแฟ (correct but stiff)	ชอบกาแฟมากเลย (Really like coffee—natural.)
I missed the train.	ฉันพลาดรถไฟ (Too literal.)	ไปไม่ทันรถไฟ (Didn't make it in time.)

Self-Reflection Quiz: Are You Stuck in the Translation Trap?

Take this **short self-reflection** quiz to see how often you translate in your head instead of thinking in Thai.

Answer YES or NO to the following:

1. **Do you pause to mentally translate before speaking Thai?**
2. **Have you ever said something in Thai and gotten a weird look in response?**
3. **Do you get stuck mid-sentence because you can't find the exact Thai word for an English thought?**
4. **Do you try to translate idioms from English into Thai (e.g., "It's raining cats and dogs") and expect them to make sense?**
5. **Do you feel more comfortable reading Thai than speaking it because you have time to translate?**

If you answered "YES" to three or more of these, you're still thinking in English first.

But don't worry—**this book is going to fix that.**

Now that you understand why **word-for-word translation is a trap,** the next step is to **train your brain to process Thai differently.**

Think about how you speak your native language. When someone asks, **"What's up?"**, you don't break it down into individual words—**you just recognize the phrase instantly** and respond automatically.

That's exactly how native Thai speakers think. Instead of translating every word, their brain retrieves **pre-built word chunks** that flow naturally in conversation.

So how do you train your brain to do the same?

In the next section, I'll introduce **the 'Chunking' Method**—a fluency hack that will rewire your brain to **think in Thai faster than ever.**

THE 'CHUNKING' METHOD FOR FASTER THINKING

Why Native Speakers Don't Think Word by Word

Imagine you're learning to play the guitar.

You wouldn't memorize each individual **finger movement** before playing a song—you'd learn **chords** (pre-built hand positions) that you can use instantly without thinking.

That's exactly how native Thai speakers **think in phrases, not words.**

Instead of translating word by word, their brain retrieves **pre-built "chunks" of language,** making their speech smooth and **instantaneous.**

Fluent Thai speakers don't say:

- *"I... want... to... go... to... the... store."*

Instead, their brain automatically recalls the chunk:

- "อยากไปตลาด" *(I want to go to the market.)*

Their brain processes the entire phrase **as a single unit, without breaking it down into individual words**—just like how you say **"What's up?"** in English without analyzing each word separately.

This is called **chunking,** and it's the key to **thinking in Thai naturally.**

Why Chunking is the Secret to Fast Thinking in Thai

Most learners struggle with fluency because they **construct sentences from scratch** every time they speak.

Here's how the typical Thai learner **forms a sentence:**

1. **Think in English first.**
   "I need to buy a ticket."

2. **Find Thai words for each one.**
   "I need" = "ฉันต้องการ"
   "to buy" = "ซื้อ"
   "a ticket" = "ตั๋ว"

3. **Translate everything in their head.**
   "ฉันต้องการซื้อตั๋ว"

4. **Finally say it (slowly, awkwardly, and with hesitation).**

Now, compare this to how a native speaker processes the same sentence:

"ต้องซื้อตั๋ว"

They don't construct it word-by-word. They just **recall the whole phrase as a chunk.**

The faster your brain recognizes and recalls chunks, the faster you'll speak Thai.

5 Essential Thai Chunks You Should Memorize Right Now

Chunk #1: "ช่วย + [verb] + หน่อยได้ไหม?" (Can you [verb] for me?)

Example Uses:

- ช่วยหยิบให้หน่อยได้ไหม? *(Can you grab it for me?)*
- ช่วยบอกเวลาหน่อยได้ไหม? *(Can you tell me the time?)*
- ช่วยอธิบายหน่อยได้ไหม? *(Can you explain it to me?)*

Why It Works:

- **High-frequency structure** (used daily).
- Works in **dozens of situations**—just swap out the verb!

Chunk #2: "กำลังจะ + [verb]" (I'm about to [do something])

Example Uses:

- กำลังจะกินข้าว *(I'm about to eat.)*
- กำลังจะออกไปข้างนอก *(I'm about to go out.)*
- กำลังจะโทรหาเธอ *(I was just about to call you.)*

Why It Works:

- **Helps you express future actions quickly** without worrying about conjugations.
- **Same pattern every time**—just swap out the verb.

Chunk #3: "อยู่ที่ไหน?" (Where is it?)

Example Uses:

- ห้องน้ำอยู่ที่ไหน? *(Where's the bathroom?)*
- ร้านกาแฟอยู่ที่ไหน? *(Where's the café?)*
- มือถือฉันอยู่ที่ไหน? *(Where's my phone?)*

Why It Works:

- Essential for **travel, everyday life, and emergencies.**
- Easy to **plug in any noun** without thinking about grammar.

Chunk #4: "ไม่แน่ใจว่า…" (I'm not sure if…)

Example Uses:

- ไม่แน่ใจว่าจะไปได้ไหม *(I'm not sure if I can go.)*
- ไม่แน่ใจว่าเขามาหรือเปล่า *(Not sure if he's coming.)*
- ไม่แน่ใจว่าดีไหม *(Not sure if it's a good idea.)*

Why It Works:

- Gives you a native way to express **uncertainty.**
- Sounds **more fluent** than just saying "ไม่รู้."

Chunk #5: "คือว่า..." (The thing is...)

Example Uses:

- คือว่าฉันติดงาน *(The thing is, I have work.)*
- คือว่าไม่มีเงินสด *(The thing is, I don't have cash.)*
- คือว่ายังไม่เข้าใจ *(The thing is, I still don't understand.)*

Why It Works:

- **Filler phrase that makes you sound more natural.**
- Gives you time to think **while keeping the conversation flowing.**

Daily Speaking Drill: The "Chunk Master" Exercise

To **train your brain to recall Thai chunks instantly,** follow this **simple daily drill:**

Step 1: Pick 5 Chunks to Focus On

Choose **5 Thai chunks** (like the ones above).

Step 2: Say Them Out Loud 10 Times

Repetition makes them **automatic.**

Step 3: Use Each Chunk in a Sentence

Come up with **a new example sentence** for each one.

Step 4: Use Them in a Real Conversation

- Talk to a native speaker.
- Use them in **language exchanges.**
- If no one is around, **say them out loud to yourself.**

Now that you know how **chunking makes Thai thinking faster, the next step is to eliminate hesitation completely** by training your brain to respond **automatically.**

EXERCISES TO REDUCE DEPENDENCY ON ENGLISH

How I Finally Stopped Thinking in English

For months, I had been stuck in **translation mode.** Every time I wanted to say something in Thai, my brain would go through this exhausting process:

1. Think of a sentence in English.
2. Translate it into Thai, word by word.
3. Get stuck trying to remember the correct verb tense.
4. Overthink if my sentence was grammatically correct.
5. Finally say something—**10 seconds too late.**

I knew this was killing my fluency, but I couldn't stop.

One day, I decided to **force my brain into Thai mode.**

For an entire week, **I eliminated English from my thoughts and daily activities** as much as possible. It felt strange at first, but by the end of the week, something clicked:

✓ **I stopped translating.**
✓ **I started understanding Thai instantly.**
✓ **I could respond faster in conversations.**

This section is going to show you how to do the same.

3 Exercises to Stop Thinking in English

Each of these exercises will **rewire your brain** to process Thai as its **own language,** not just an English translation.

They are structured as a **7-day fluency plan,** helping you **gradually shift your brain into Thai mode.**

Exercise #1: Train Your Inner Monologue in Thai

Most people don't realize that they **think in their native language all day long.**

If you can **train your inner monologue to be in Thai,** you will:

- ✓ **Reduce your dependency on English.**
- ✓ **Learn to recall Thai words faster.**
- ✓ **Build fluency even when you're not speaking.**

How It Works (Day 1-3)

Step 1: Narrate Simple Thoughts in Thai

- As you go about your day, describe **everything you see** in Thai.
- Example: Instead of thinking, *"I need to find my keys,"* say in your head: "ต้องหากุญแจให้เจอ"

Step 2: Narrate Your Daily Routine

- As you wake up, **mentally describe everything you do:** ตื่นนอน → ล้างหน้า → ชงกาแฟ → ออกไปทำงาน *(Wake up. Wash my face. Make coffee. Leave for work.)*

Step 3: Use a "Thai Only" Thinking Period

- Choose **one hour per day** where you force yourself to **only think in Thai.**
- If you don't know a word, **describe it in Thai** instead of translating.

Example:

- Instead of thinking *"What's the word for 'ceiling'?"*
- Think: **"คือส่วนบนของห้อง"** *(It's the top part of a room.)*

By Day 3, your brain will **start forming thoughts in Thai naturally.**

Exercise #2: Speak to Yourself in Thai About Daily Activities

Now that your **thoughts** are in Thai, it's time to **train your speech.**

This will teach you to **recall Thai words instantly**—without hesitation.

How It Works (Day 4-6)

Step 1: Describe Your Surroundings Out Loud

- Whenever you're alone, **speak in Thai about what you see.**
- Example: If you're walking down the street, say: "กำลังเดินอยู่ที่ถนน มีร้านเยอะเลย ท้องฟ้าสดใส" *(I'm walking down the street. There are many shops. The sky is clear.)*

Step 2: "Daily Recap" Speaking Challenge

- Every night, **summarize your day in Thai out loud**—as if you were telling a friend.
- Example: "วันนี้ไปทำงาน งานยุ่งมาก แต่หลังเลิกงานไปออกกำลังกาย แล้วทานข้าวกับครอบครัว ดูซีรีส์ไทยก่อนนอน" *(Today I went to work. It was super busy, but afterward, I worked out, had dinner with family, and watched a Thai series before bed.)*

Step 3: Shadowing Practice

- Pick a Thai **YouTube video or podcast.**
- Listen to **one sentence at a time** and immediately repeat it **out loud**—without stopping.
- **Mimic the speed, tone, and pronunciation of the speaker.**

By Day 6, you'll be able to **speak in Thai faster and more naturally.**

Exercise #3: Test Yourself in a Full Thai Conversation

Now that you **think and talk to yourself in Thai,** it's time for **the final challenge:**

Have a full conversation in Thai—no English allowed.

How It Works (Day 7)

Step 1: Find a Speaking Partner

- Join a **language exchange app** (Tandem, HelloTalk, or iTalki).
- Find a Thai speaker and **schedule a 15-minute conversation.**

Step 2: Use Chunks Instead of Translating

- Focus on using **pre-built phrases (chunks)** instead of constructing sentences from English.
- Example:
  - Instead of thinking *"How do I say 'I think it's interesting'?"*
  - Just recall the chunk: **"รู้สึกว่าน่าสนใจ"**

Step 3: Force Yourself to Keep Talking

- If you forget a word, **describe it in Thai** instead of switching to English.
- Example: Instead of **stopping** because you forgot *"furniture"*, say: **"ของที่อยู่ในบ้าน เช่น เก้าอี้ โต๊ะ ตู้"** *(Things that are in a house, like chairs, tables, cabinets.)*

Step 4: Record Yourself Speaking

- After the conversation, **record yourself talking about any topic for 2 minutes.**
- Compare it to your first attempt at speaking Thai—**you'll notice a huge improvement!**

By the end of this exercise, your brain will **no longer rely on English**—you'll be thinking, speaking, and responding in Thai **automatically.**

7-Day "No English" Training Plan

Day	Exercise
Day 1	Train your **inner monologue** in Thai.
Day 2	Narrate your **daily routine** in Thai.
Day 3	Think in Thai for **1 full hour** (no English allowed).
Day 4	Describe your **surroundings out loud** in Thai.
Day 5	Recap your **day in Thai** (speak for 1-2 minutes).
Day 6	**Shadow a native speaker** (repeat phrases instantly).
Day 7	Have a **full Thai conversation with no English.**

Now that you've eliminated English from your thinking, the next step is to **train your brain to react in Thai without hesitation.**

If you've ever frozen mid-conversation, struggling to find the right words, it's because your brain **isn't used to responding at full speed.**

In Chapter 3, we'll introduce **powerful fluency drills** designed to **force instant Thai responses—no time to think, no time to translate.**

Your Thai fluency is about to take a giant leap forward—let's go!

CHAPTER THREE:
Building Automatic Responses

THE MOMENT I FINALLY STARTED THINKING IN THAI

I was half-asleep when it happened.

It was late at night in Chiang Mai, and I was lying in my Airbnb bed, exhausted from a long day of exploring temples, sipping iced coffee, and dodging motorbikes in the old city. The street outside buzzed with life—motorcycles passing, distant laughter, the occasional bark of a soi dog. The warm air carried the smell of grilled pork skewers and sticky rice, and I could still taste the sweet chili sauce from dinner.

My phone buzzed on the nightstand.

I lazily reached for it, squinting at the screen. A message from my local friend, Napat:

- "พรุ่งนี้เจอกันกี่โมงดี?"

Half-conscious, I stared at the message. Normally, my brain would have **gone into full processing mode:**

1. *Okay... "พรุ่งนี้" means "tomorrow."*
2. *"เจอกันกี่โมง"... that's "what time will we meet?"*
3. *So... he's asking, "What time should we meet tomorrow?"*

But this time, something strange happened.

There was no translation. No mental breakdown of each word. No hesitation.

I just understood it—instantly.

Before I even realized what I was doing, my fingers typed back:

- "สักแปดโมงก็ได้" *(Eight is fine.)*

And then, as if nothing significant had just happened, I put my phone down and rolled over.

It wasn't until the next morning, while brushing my teeth, that it hit me.

Wait... I didn't translate that. I didn't overthink it. I just... responded.

For the first time in my life, my brain had **processed Thai directly, without using English as a middleman.**

I had crossed over.

I was **thinking in Thai.**

The Fluency "Switch"

If you've ever struggled to **speak Thai quickly,** it's because your brain is still treating it like **a school subject** rather than a language.

Here's what's happening inside your head:

Before the "Switch" (Translation Mode):

- Someone asks you a question in Thai.
- Your brain translates it into English first.
- You think of an answer in English.
- You translate your answer back into Thai.
- You finally respond—too late, too slow, and too robotic.

After the "Switch" (Automatic Thinking Mode):

- Someone asks you a question in Thai.
- Your brain **processes it instantly**—without translating.
- You respond **naturally, like a native speaker.**

At this stage, **Thai is no longer a foreign language—it's just a different way your brain processes thoughts.**

This chapter is going to show you **exactly how to reach that point.**

Because once you do? Speaking Thai will feel **as natural as breathing.**

In this chapter, I'll show you:

✓ **How to train your brain to respond in Thai instantly.**
✓ **Drills that will force your brain to stop translating and start reacting naturally.**
✓ **Techniques native speakers use to process language automatically.**

We're not just going to talk about fluency—we're going to **train for it.**

By the end of this chapter, you won't just understand Thai—you'll be **thinking in it.**

Let's go.

THE 'NO TIME TO TRANSLATE' DRILL

Why Thinking Slower = Speaking Slower

Imagine this: You're at a café in Bangkok. The waiter walks up and asks:

- **"จะดื่มอะไรดีคะ?"** *(Would you like something to drink?)*

Your brain **freezes.** You start analyzing:

- *"จะดื่ม" = will drink...*
- *"อะไร" = what...*
- *"ดี" = good...*
- *So she's asking, "What would you like to drink?"*

By the time you've processed all this, the waiter is already **taking someone else's order.**

Meanwhile, a native Thai speaker would have **responded in less than a second:**

- **"กาแฟค่ะ"** *(Coffee, please.)*

What's the difference?

Native speakers **don't think word by word**—they hear the phrase, recognize the meaning **instantly,** and respond **automatically.**

The **No Time to Translate Drill** will **train your brain to do the same.**

What is the 'No Time to Translate' Drill?

This drill forces you to **respond in Thai immediately,** so your brain **stops relying on English** and starts **thinking in Thai naturally.**

It works because:

✓ **It speeds up your brain's response time.**
✓ **It eliminates hesitation caused by overthinking.**
✓ **It forces you to retrieve words instantly, like a native speaker.**

By practicing **this drill daily,** you'll **cut translation out of your thinking process** and start responding instantly.

Step-by-Step Guide to the No Time to Translate Drill

Phase 1: Instant One-Word Answers (Days 1-2)

Goal: Train your brain to respond with a **single Thai word immediately.**

How it works:

- Have a friend or language partner ask you **super simple questions.**
- You **must answer within 1 second**—no hesitation.

Example Questions & Instant Answers:

Question	Fast Response
กาแฟหรือชา? *(Coffee or tea?)*	กาแฟ
ทะเลหรือภูเขา? *(Beach or mountains?)*	ทะเล
เช้าหรือบ่าย? *(Morning or afternoon?)*	เช้า

Progression Tip:

If you hesitate, repeat the drill **faster and faster** until your brain automatically fires off answers.

Phase 2: Short Sentence Responses (Days 3-5)

Goal: Expand to 3-4 word responses.

How it works:

- Instead of **one-word answers, add a little detail.**
- Still respond **within 1 second**—no pausing!

Example Questions & Short Responses:

Question	Fast Response
สบายดีไหม? *(How are you?)*	สบายดี ขอบคุณค่ะ
ทำอะไรอยู่? *(What are you doing?)*	กำลังทำงานอยู่
อยากกินอะไร? *(What do you want to eat?)*	อยากกินก๋วยเตี๋ยว

Progression Tip:

If you pause, **use a filler phrase** like:

- ไม่แน่ใจนะ... *(Not sure...)*
- ขอคิดก่อน... *(Let me think...)*

This will help you **avoid silence** while your brain catches up.

Phase 3: Full Conversation Mode (Days 6-7)

Goal: Respond in **complete sentences** without thinking in English.

How it works:

- Have a friend **ask you random questions.**
- You must **respond in full Thai sentences instantly.**

Example Questions & Full Responses:

Question	Fast Response
เมื่อวานทำอะไร? *(What did you do yesterday?)*	ไปดูหนังกับเพื่อนมาค่ะ *(Went to the movies with friends.)*
เมืองคุณเป็นยังไง? *(What's your city like?)*	เมืองใหญ่มากแล้วก็มีประวัติศาสตร์เยอะ *(Big and full of history.)*
ทำงานอะไร? *(What do you do for work?)*	เป็นนักออกแบบกราฟิกในบริษัทค่ะ *(I'm a graphic designer at a company.)*

Final Challenge:

By **Day 7,** you should be able to:

- ✓ Respond in Thai **instantly.**
- ✓ Keep conversations **flowing without pausing.**
- ✓ Stop translating in your head **completely.**

Bonus: The Audio Challenge (Train Your Brain to Respond Instantly)

Listening and **responding instantly to spoken Thai** is key to fluency.

How it works:

- **Find an audio clip of native Thai speech** (YouTube, podcasts, Netflix).
- **Pause after each sentence.**
- **Say the first response that comes to mind**—without overthinking.

Example Scenario (Audio Clip):

Thai Speaker: "นัดเจอกันกี่โมงดี?" *(What time should we meet?)*
Your Brain: (No translation, just answer!)
You Say: "สักหนึ่งทุ่มก็ดีค่ะ" *(Around 7PM is fine.)*

Thai Speaker: "ชอบอาหารไทยไหม?" *(Do you like Thai food?)*
Your Brain: (No English, just respond!)
You Say: "ชอบมากค่ะ" *(I love it.)*

The goal is to **respond naturally,** without pausing to analyze.

7-Day "No Time to Translate" Training Plan

Day	Exercise
Day 1	**One-word responses only.** Answer within **1 second.**
Day 2	Repeat **one-word response drill,** but **increase speed.**
Day 3	Expand to **short 3-4 word answers.**
Day 4	**Short sentence responses,** no pauses.
Day 5	**Practice full Thai sentences** instantly.
Day 6	**Have a real conversation** (no English allowed).
Day 7	**Do the Audio Challenge**—respond instantly to native speech.

Now that your brain is **firing off responses instantly,** it's time to **supercharge your fluency speed** even further.

In the next section, I'll introduce **The Shadowing Technique**—a powerful method used by **language learners and interpreters** to train **real-time fluency.**

Your Thai is **getting faster and smoother**—let's go!

THE SHADOWING TECHNIQUE – MIMIC LIKE A NATIVE

The Secret to Sounding Fluent Without Thinking

I once watched a YouTube video of a polyglot who spoke **10 languages** fluently.

I expected him to say that he had spent **years studying grammar** or that he had **memorized thousands of flashcards.**

But instead, he said something surprising:

"I don't learn languages—I imitate them."

He explained that the fastest way to **think and speak fluently** in any language is to **shadow native speakers**—literally **mimic their speech in real time.**

That's when I discovered the **Shadowing Technique**—a powerful method that can **rewire your brain to think in Thai without hesitation.**

If you've ever struggled with:

- **Hesitating before speaking**
- **Thinking in English first**
- **Translating in your head before responding**

…then **Shadowing** is the technique that will change everything.

What is the Shadowing Technique?

Shadowing is a training method where you **listen to a native Thai speaker and repeat what they say instantly—without pausing or thinking.**

This technique forces your brain to:

- ✓ **Process Thai in real time** (like a native speaker).
- ✓ **Eliminate hesitation and overthinking.**
- ✓ **Mimic pronunciation, rhythm, and intonation perfectly.**

Think of it as **language weightlifting**—you're **training your mouth, brain, and ears** to work together at full speed.

After just **one week** of Shadowing, you'll notice:

- ✓ Faster responses in conversations
- ✓ More natural pronunciation
- ✓ Less mental effort when speaking

Step-by-Step Guide to the Shadowing Technique

Step 1: Choose the Right Thai Audio

Not all Thai audio is **ideal for Shadowing.** You need:

- ✓ **Native speakers** (avoid robotic voices).
- ✓ **Clear and natural speech** (not too slow, not too fast).
- ✓ **Everyday conversational Thai** (not formal news broadcasts).

Best Types of Audio for Shadowing:

- **Thai Podcasts** (Intermediate level)
- **YouTube videos** (With subtitles)
- **Thai Audiobooks** (Easy listening)
- **Thai TV Series or Lakorns** (Dialogues with emotions and natural rhythm)

Pro Tip: Use **Thai subtitles** when possible to **connect sound with text.**

Step 2: Listen & Repeat – No Pausing!

Press Play & Listen

- Choose a **short clip (30-60 seconds).**
- Play it once **without stopping** to absorb the rhythm.

Repeat Immediately

- Play it again, and **speak at the same time as the speaker.**
- Don't stop, even if you **don't understand every word.**
- Focus on **mimicking pronunciation, speed, and intonation.**

Use 'Echo Shadowing'

- If the audio is too fast, **repeat with a 1-second delay** behind the speaker.
- Gradually speed up until you **match them exactly.**

Why This Works: Your brain **stops analyzing and starts reacting instantly**—just like in real conversations.

Step 3: Increase the Difficulty

Once you master **basic shadowing,** push yourself further:

Level 1: Slow & Clear Speech

- **Use beginner-friendly podcasts or slow Thai dialogues.**
- **Repeat every word clearly.**

Level 2: Conversational Thai

- **Use YouTube videos with native speakers.**
- **Mimic their rhythm & expressions.**

Level 3: Rapid Native Speech (Advanced Mode!)

- **Use fast-paced Thai TV shows or real conversations.**
- **Match their speed & pronunciation exactly.**

Pro Tip: If a phrase is too hard, **repeat it 10 times until it feels natural.**

Recommended Thai Resources for Shadowing

Here's a list of the **best materials** to practice shadowing:

Podcasts (Slow & Clear Thai)

- **Learn Thai Gluay Gluay** (Beginner-friendly)
- **ThaiPod101** (Wide range of levels)
- **BananaThai Podcast** (Everyday Thai with explanations)

YouTube Channels (Everyday Thai)

- **Thai with Grace** (Practical and clear)
- **Learn Thai with Mod** (Conversational Thai)
- **PickupThai** (Natural Thai dialogues and culture)

Audiobooks (Easy Listening)

- **Thai Fairy Tales** (for kids and adults alike)
- **69 Short Thai Stories for Beginners** (Perfect for shadowing)

TV Shows (Fast-Paced Speech)

- **Hormones** (Teen drama, fast and emotional)
- **Bangkok Breaking** (Everyday speech, slang-heavy)
- **Girl From Nowhere** (Fast but well-enunciated)

Pro Tip: Start with **slow Thai audio,** then **gradually increase speed.**

Shadowing Fluency Challenge: 7-Day Plan

Goal: Train your brain to **process & speak Thai instantly.**

Day	Exercise
Day 1	Shadow a **slow Thai podcast** for 5 minutes.
Day 2	Shadow **a YouTube video** (with subtitles).
Day 3	Shadow **without subtitles** (force your brain to rely on listening).
Day 4	Shadow a **TV show dialogue** (repeat multiple times).
Day 5	Shadow **a real Thai conversation** (from a podcast or show).
Day 6	Shadow **at full speed** (no pausing, match the native speaker).
Day 7	Shadow **a live conversation** (e.g., listen to locals talking in a café).

By the end of the week, your speech will be FASTER and MORE NATURAL.

Now that you've learned to **shadow Thai like a native speaker,** the next step is to **train your brain to react instantly in real conversations.**

In the next section, I'll introduce the **3-Second Fluency Response**—a powerful technique to **eliminate hesitation and build natural, confident speech.**

3-SECOND FLUENCY RESPONSE GAME

Why Fast Responses = Fluency

Think about the last time someone asked you a question in Thai.

Did you:

- **Pause and think about how to translate your response?**
- **Get stuck trying to remember the right verb tense?**
- **Hesitate so long that the conversation moved on without you?**

If so, you're not alone. Most Thai learners **freeze** in conversations because they're trying to construct the perfect sentence **instead of responding instinctively.**

But guess what? **Fluency isn't about perfection—it's about speed.**

Native speakers **don't plan every sentence** before they speak. Their brain automatically pulls up the **right phrases in real time**—like muscle memory.

The **3-Second Fluency Response Game** will train your brain to do the same.

What is the 3-Second Fluency Response Game?

This is a **high-speed speaking drill** that forces you to:

- ✓ **Think in Thai instead of translating.**
- ✓ **Respond instantly, without overthinking.**
- ✓ **Keep talking, even if you make mistakes.**

The rule is simple:

You must answer every question within 3 seconds.

If you hesitate, you lose. If you keep going, you build fluency.

How to Play the 3-Second Fluency Response Game

Phase 1: Fast & Simple Responses (Days 1-2)

Goal: Train your brain to respond with **short answers instantly.**

1. Look at a **basic Thai question.**
2. Set a **3-second timer.**
3. Say your answer **out loud, without hesitating.**

Example Questions & Instant Answers:

Question	Fast Response
คุณชื่ออะไร? *(What's your name?)*	ผมชื่อต้นครับ / ฉันชื่อน้ำค่ะ
คุณมาจากที่ไหน? *(Where are you from?)*	ผมมาจากกรุงเทพฯ / ฉันมาจากเชียงใหม่
คุณมีพี่น้องไหม? *(Do you have siblings?)*	มีค่ะ / ครับ มีน้องชายหนึ่งคน

Speed Challenge: If you hesitate, **repeat the drill faster and faster** until your brain reacts instantly.

Phase 2: Full Sentence Responses (Days 3-4)

Goal: Expand to **longer, natural-sounding responses.**

How it works:

- Instead of **one-word answers,** give **a full sentence.**
- Keep responding **within 3 seconds**—no pausing!

Example Questions & Longer Responses:

Question	Fast Response
เมื่อวานคุณทำอะไร? *(What did you do yesterday?)*	เมื่อวานฉันไปดูหนังกับเพื่อน ดูหนังแอ็กชันสนุกมาก
เมืองของคุณเป็นยังไง? *(What's your city like?)*	เมืองฉันใหญ่ มีตลาดนัดเยอะ แล้วก็ของกินเยอะมาก
คุณชอบอาหารอะไรที่สุด? *(What's your favorite food?)*	ฉันชอบกินก๋วยเตี๋ยว โดยเฉพาะแบบต้มยำ

Fluency Tip: If you **can't think of the perfect sentence,** just say **anything** that fits. Don't stop talking.

Phase 3: Full Conversation Mode (Days 5-6)

Goal: Maintain a **flowing Thai conversation** with no hesitation.

How it works:

- Have a **friend, tutor, or language partner** ask you rapid-fire questions.
- You **must keep talking for 30 seconds per response**—no pauses allowed!

Example Questions for Full Conversations:

Question	Example Extended Response
สุดสัปดาห์ที่ผ่านมาเป็นยังไง? *(How was your weekend?)*	สนุกมาก วันเสาร์ไปงานเลี้ยงกับเพื่อน วันอาทิตย์ก็นอนดูซีรีส์ที่บ้าน
ปกติคุณชอบทำอะไรเวลาว่าง? *(What do you usually do in your free time?)*	ฉันชอบอ่านหนังสือภาษาไทย ฟังเพลง แล้วก็เดินเล่นที่สวนสาธารณะ
วันปกติของคุณเป็นยังไงบ้าง? *(What's a typical day like for you?)*	ตอนเช้าตื่นแต่เช้า ออกกำลังกาย กินข้าวเช้า แล้วก็ทำงาน ตอนเย็นเรียนภาษาไทย

Advanced Mode: Try answering **without using English at all** in your mind.

Phase 4: Thai-Only Conversation Challenge (Day 7)

Goal: Have a **full 5-minute conversation in Thai—no English allowed.**

How it works:

- Find a **language exchange partner or tutor.**
- Set a **5-minute timer.**
- You must **talk continuously in Thai**—even if you struggle.

Rules:

- **No English.** If you don't know a word, describe it in Thai.
- **Keep talking.** If you get stuck, use filler phrases like:
  - เอ่อ... (Uhh...)
  - ขอคิดแป๊บนึง... (Let me think...)
  - มันเหมือนกับว่า... (It's kind of like...)
- **React quickly.** If your partner asks a question, respond **within 3 seconds.**

By the end of this challenge, you'll be speaking Thai naturally—without hesitation.

Day	Exercise
Day 1	Answer **basic questions** within **3 seconds.**
Day 2	Repeat **one-word response drill** at a faster speed.
Day 3	Expand to **full-sentence responses** within 3 seconds.
Day 4	**Have a 3-minute conversation** with no hesitation.
Day 5	Answer **longer questions** in full detail.
Day 6	**Practice full-speed dialogue** with a partner.
Day 7	**Have a full 5-minute Thai conversation—no English allowed!**

By the end of the week, your brain will be trained to react in Thai instantly.

Now that your brain is **firing off Thai responses in real time,** the next step is to **train your inner voice to think in Thai—even when you're not speaking.**

In Chapter 4, **we'll dive into how native Thai speakers structure their thoughts differently from English speakers.**

Instead of thinking in English and translating, you'll learn to **rearrange your thoughts the way a Thai speaker would—naturally and effortlessly.**

Your Thai fluency is reaching the next level—let's go!

CHAPTER FOUR:
Developing Thought Patterns in Thai

THE TIME I ACCIDENTALLY INSULTED A LANDLORD IN THAILAND

It all started with a simple apartment viewing in Bangkok.

I had been in Thailand for a few weeks, and I was finally ready to stop living out of budget hotels and find a place of my own. After browsing some Thai property apps, I found a promising listing—a cozy studio right near the BTS Skytrain and just minutes from some great street food stalls. The photos looked amazing, the price was reasonable, and the description even boasted "มีแสงธรรมชาติเยอะ" (a lot of natural light). It seemed perfect.

So, I scheduled a viewing with the landlord, **Khun Prasert,** a serious-looking man in his late 50s who had the expression of someone who had seen far too many bad tenants in his lifetime.

We met outside the building, exchanged a polite handshake, and rode the tiny, creaky elevator up to the third floor.

"This is it," he said, unlocking the door with a dramatic sigh, as if revealing a luxury penthouse instead of a 28-square-meter studio.

I stepped inside, nodding, trying to look professional and experienced—like someone who definitely knew what he was doing in the Bangkok rental market.

But as soon as I looked around, I realized something was… off.

Yes, it had a lot of **"natural light"**—because the curtains were completely missing. The walls had that faint gray tint you see in apartments that have survived multiple rainy seasons. And in the middle of the room stood **the world's smallest fridge**—I'm talking **hotel minibar size.**

But I wasn't going to be rude. I wanted to be polite, professional, and **sound fluent.**

So, I decided to say something simple. Something neutral.

- "I like it."

Unfortunately, I had **not yet mastered Thai sentence structure.** And in my head, I simply took the English phrase **"I like it"** and translated it word-for-word into Thai.

So I looked at Khun Prasert, smiled, and confidently said:

- **"ฉันชอบมันค่ะ"**

Silence.

His expression didn't change. He blinked at me. Twice.

That was when I felt the first wave of panic hit.

Something was wrong.

Very, very wrong.

I had **no idea what I had just said,** but it clearly wasn't the Thai equivalent of "I like it."

Khun Prasert narrowed his eyes slightly and tilted his head, the way you do when someone says something so **confusingly stupid** that you're trying to decide whether to correct them or just pretend it never happened.

Then, after a long pause, he sighed and muttered:

- **"อืม...โอเคครับ"** (Umm... okay.)

And just like that, he continued the tour.

I nodded along, pretending I hadn't just **accidentally said something bizarre** to my potential landlord.

I spent the rest of the visit distracted, my brain frantically trying to **decode what I had just said** and why it **clearly** wasn't right.

It wasn't until I left the apartment, took out my phone, and searched **"I like it" in Thai** that I finally realized my mistake. The correct way would've been something like:

- **"ดูดีนะครับ"** (It looks nice) **or "ห้องน่าอยู่ดีครับ"** (This place looks livable/cozy).

But what I had said—**"ฉันชอบมัน"**—was technically grammatically okay, but it sounded robotic, overly direct, and kind of… unnatural. Like something a student would say during a Thai oral exam, not in real life.

It was like if someone learning English walked into your house, looked around, and proudly declared:

- **"I enjoy it, yes."**

Awkward.

That was the moment I realized something critical: **thinking in English and translating word-for-word into Thai was a recipe for disaster.**

And that's exactly what this chapter is about.

Up until now, we've been focused on breaking the habit of translating every sentence in your head. But to truly think in Thai, you have to go a step further:

You need to **restructure your thoughts** to match **how Thai speakers think**—not just swap out English words for Thai ones.

In this chapter, we're going to:

- ✓ **Break down how Thai sentence structure affects thinking**
- ✓ **Rewire your brain to form sentences in Thai order automatically**
- ✓ **Train your brain to stop relying on English structures**

By the end of this chapter, you won't just **speak** Thai—you'll **think like a Thai speaker.**

Let's get started.

HOW THAI SENTENCE STRUCTURE AFFECTS THINKING

Thai is not just a different set of vocabulary—it's a **completely different way of structuring thoughts.** If you keep trying to think in English and just swap in Thai words, you'll end up with sentences that sound unnatural, confusing, or even completely incorrect.

So how do native Thai speakers **actually think?** Let's break down the key structural differences and then **train your brain** to process Thai the right way.

Why Word-for-Word Translation Doesn't Work

Imagine you're in a café in Chiang Mai, and you want to ask someone:

- "**Do you have a car?**"

Your English-trained brain might try to **directly translate each word:**

× "คุณ ทำ มี รถ ไหม?" (Nope. This makes no sense.)

Here's how a Thai speaker actually says it:

✓ "คุณมีรถไหม?" (Literally: "You have car, question particle?")

In English, we rely on the **helping verb 'do'** to form questions (**Do you like coffee?**). But Thai doesn't use this structure at all. Instead, it places the verb directly and uses polite or questioning particles to show tone.

- **Do you like coffee?** → "คุณชอบกาแฟไหม?" (Literally: "You like coffee?")
- **Do you speak Thai?** → "คุณพูดภาษาไทยได้ไหม?" (Literally: "You speak Thai can?")

The Thai brain **does not think in extra words** like "do"—it **jumps straight to the core idea.**

Thai Sentences Follow a Different Order

Think of these two simple sentences:

- **"A red car."**
- "รถสีแดง"

Did you notice something? **The structure is reversed!**

In English, we say "a red car" with the adjective (red) **before the noun** (car). But in Thai, the noun (car) comes first, **then** the color (red):

- **A blue house** → "บ้านสีฟ้า"
- **A big dog** → "หมาตัวใหญ่"
- **A delicious pizza** → "พิซซ่าอร่อย"

How This Changes Your Thinking:

When describing something in Thai, you need to picture the object first, then its qualities—just like a native Thai speaker.

- **English thinking:** "I want to buy a small black cat."
- **Thai thinking:** "I want to buy a cat small black." → "ฉันอยากซื้อแมวสีดำตัวเล็ก"

Reflexive & Passive-Like Expressions: When Thai Shifts the Blame

Thai often uses constructions that shift focus away from the subject, especially when something bad happens. Look at this:

- **"I forgot."** (Standard English sentence.)
- "ลืมไปแล้ว" **or** "ฉันลืม" (Literally: "Forgot already" or "I forgot")

But if you want to say "I forgot my keys," it often becomes:

- "ลืมกุญแจไว้" **or** "ลืมกุญแจที่บ้าน" (Forgot keys at home)

Or if something happens to you unexpectedly:

- **"I broke the glass."** → "แก้วแตกเอง" (The glass broke by itself)
- **"She dropped the book."** → "หนังสือตกเอง" (The book fell on its own)

How This Changes Your Thinking:

Thai speakers often express situations as things that happened, not things they did. This removes blame and softens the tone—very culturally Thai.

Training Exercises: Rewiring Your Brain to Think in Thai

Now that you understand the key **structural differences**, let's rewire your brain with **three powerful exercises**.

Exercise #1: "Drop the 'Do'" Question Challenge

How it works: Convert these English questions into **natural Thai** without using the word "do."

× **English:** Do you like mangoes?
✓ **Thai:** คุณชอบมะม่วงไหม?

Try these:

1. **Do you have a car? → ___________?**
2. **Do you speak Thai? → ___________?**
3. **Do they know the answer? → ___________?**
4. **Does she live here? → ___________?**
5. **Do we need more time? → ___________?**

Exercise #2: "Reverse the Adjective" Drill

How it works: Rewrite these English descriptions in Thai with the adjective or quality after the noun.

- × **English:** A beautiful city
- ✓ **Thai:** เมืองสวย

Try these:

1. **A big house → ___________**
2. **A difficult test → ___________**
3. **A friendly person → ___________**
4. **A long movie → ___________**
5. **A delicious cake → ___________**

Exercise #3: "Think Like Thai" Exercise

How it works: Convert these English sentences into natural Thai phrasing, using passive or neutral language when appropriate.

- × **English:** I forgot my wallet.
- ✓ **Thai:** ลืมกระเป๋าสตางค์ไว้

Try these:

1. **I lost my wallet. → ______________**
2. **He broke his phone. → ______________**
3. **We ran out of money. → ______________**
4. **She dropped the book. → ______________**
5. **They got sick. → ______________**

Reflection Exercise: Train Your Thoughts in Thai

Now, let's **apply everything** with a self-reflection challenge.

Instructions: Rewrite the following English thoughts in a natural **Thai structure—WITHOUT** direct translation.

- × **English:** I like the new phone.
- ✓ **Thai: ชอบโทรศัพท์ใหม่อันนี้**

Try these:

1. **I need a big suitcase. → ___________**
2. **She has a red dress. → ___________**
3. **We love Thai food. → ___________**
4. **They forgot the meeting. → ___________**
5. **I dropped my glass. → ___________**

ADJUSTING TO SUBJECT-VERB DIFFERENCES

Imagine you're at a café in Chiang Mai, and the waiter asks, "กินอะไรดีครับ?" (What would you like to eat?).

Now, if you're thinking in English, your brain might expect a more complete sentence:

× "คุณจะกินอะไร?" (You will eat what?)

But native Thai speakers don't always say the subject (you, I, he, she, we, etc.)—they just go straight to the verb and add a polite particle or context-based clue.

✓ "กินอะไรดี?" (Eat what well?/What to eat?)

No subject. No fluff. Just straight to the point.

That's because **Thai operates on a different mental structure**—one where context does a lot of the heavy lifting and where the subject is often unnecessary or implied.

This section is all about breaking free from **English subject-verb habits** and **rewiring your brain** to **think like a Thai speaker.**

Why Thai Drops the Subject

In English, we **always** need a subject:

- **I am going to the store.**
- **She likes Thai food.**
- **They are coming later.**

But in Thai, the subject is often dropped if it's obvious from context:

- ไปตลาด (Going to the market.)
- ชอบอาหารไทย (Like Thai food.)
- กำลังมา (Coming.)

Since Thai relies on context and doesn't conjugate verbs like English does, native speakers think in ideas, not full grammatical units.

Key takeaway: Thai speakers don't say what doesn't need to be said. If the subject is clear from context, they skip it and move on.

How This Changes Your Thinking:

Instead of translating "I am going to the market," your brain should skip "I" and go straight to the action:

- **English brain:** "I am going to the market."
- **Thai brain: "ไปตลาด"** (Go market.)

Challenge: Try describing what you're doing right now without using "I" or **"ฉัน"**.

The Different Word Order for Questions

Another **key difference** between English and Thai is **question structure.**

In English, we rely on **helper verbs** to form questions:

- **What do you want?**
- **Where does he live?**
- **Why are they leaving?**

Thai doesn't use helper words like **do, does,** or **are.** It just flips or reorders elements as needed:

✓ อยากได้อะไร? **(Want what?) → No "do"!**
✓ เขาอยู่ที่ไหน? **(He live where?) → No "does"!**
✓ ทำไมไปแล้ว? **(Why gone already?) → No "are"!**

Key takeaway: Thai questions are simpler. They drop unnecessary helpers and go straight to the point.

How Thai Verbs Carry More Meaning

Thai verbs may not conjugate, but they can carry plenty of meaning when paired with time words, particles, and context.

For example:

- หิวข้าว (Literally: "Hungry for rice.") → **I'm hungry**
- หนาว (Cold) → **It's cold**
- ปวดหัว (Head hurts) → **I have a headache**

Thai doesn't always use "I am…" for things like feelings or conditions. Instead, it jumps directly to the state or experience.

Key takeaway: Instead of thinking "I am hungry," train your brain to think "Hungry already" or "Hungry rice."

Training Exercises: Rewiring Your Brain for Thai Subject-Verb Thinking

Now it's time to **practice shifting your thought structure** with **three powerful drills.**

Exercise #1: Drop the Subject Challenge

How it works: Answer the following questions without using a subject (like **ฉัน**, **คุณ**, **เขา**, etc.).

- × **English-thinking answer:** "I am learning Thai."
- ✓ **Thai-thinking answer:** เรียนภาษาไทยอยู่ (Learning Thai currently.)

Try these:

1. **What do you do? → ______________?**
2. **Are you coming? → ______________?**
3. **Do you have a dog? → ______________?**
4. **Are we leaving? → ______________?**
5. **Do they speak English? → ______________?**

Exercise #2: Word Order Switch-Up Drill

How it works: Rearrange these English questions into **natural Thai order.**

- × **English-thinking:** "What do you want?"
- ✓ **Thai-thinking:** อยากได้อะไร?

Try these:

1. **Why do you study Thai? → ___________?**
2. **When does she arrive? → ___________?**
3. **How do they know that? → ___________?**
4. **Where do we go? → ___________?**
5. **What do you think? → ___________?**

Exercise #3: Verb Power Exercise

How it works: Convert these English thoughts into Thai-style expressions.

- × **English-thinking:** "I am hungry."
- ✓ **Thai-thinking:** หิวข้าว

Try these:

1. **I'm thirsty. → ___________**
2. **It's cold. → ___________**
3. **I'm afraid. → ___________**
4. **My leg hurts. → ___________**
5. **It's hot today. → ___________**

Final Challenge: Thinking in Thai Structures

Now let's **put everything together**.

Instructions: Rewrite the following English thoughts **in Thai-style structure**—WITHOUT direct translation.

- × **English-thinking:** "I don't know where she is."
- ✓ **Thai-thinking:** ไม่รู้ว่าเธออยู่ที่ไหน

Try these:

1. **They are coming later. → ___________**
2. **It's raining outside. → ___________**
3. **We are leaving now. → ___________**
4. **He needs help. → ___________**
5. **I don't have money. → ___________**

EXERCISES TO RESTRUCTURE YOUR THOUGHTS

By now, you understand that **Thai and English structure thoughts differently**. But knowing this **isn't enough**—you need to **train your brain** to think in Thai **naturally and instinctively**.

In this section, we're going to **rewire your thought process** through three powerful exercises. These drills will **force your brain** to adapt to **Thai word order, phrasing, and thought patterns**—so you can **form sentences naturally, without relying on English.**

Exercise #1: The Thai Word-Order Drill

Goal: Train your brain to **rearrange English sentence structure into natural Thai.**

Many English learners struggle because they **think in English word order** and then **try to swap in Thai words**—which leads to unnatural sentences.

Example:

- × **English-thinking:** "I like that red car."
- × **Direct translation:** ฉัน ชอบ นั้น รถ สีแดง (Wrong.)
- ✓ **Natural Thai:** ฉันชอบรถสีแดงคันนั้น ("I like the red car that one.")

How the Drill Works:

1. Look at an English sentence.
2. Rearrange it in **Thai order** (without translating it yet).
3. Say the Thai sentence out loud.

Try it with these:

- **She bought a blue dress. →** ___________
- **We need a bigger table. →** ___________
- **They have an interesting book. →** ___________
- **I love small towns. →** ___________
- **Can you give me the red notebook? →** ___________

Pro Tip: Picture the Thai words in your mind instead of imagining the English sentence first.

Exercise #2: The 'Reverse Translation' Exercise

Goal: Stop relying on English translations and start thinking in **Thai meaning.**

Many learners make the mistake of **seeing a Thai phrase** and immediately **trying to convert it into English**. But native speakers **don't translate**—they just **understand the meaning** directly.

How the Drill Works:

1. Look at a Thai sentence.
2. Instead of translating it into English, **describe its meaning** using **only Thai words.**
3. Focus on **explaining the idea**, not just swapping words.

Example:

- ▹ **Thai:** ฉันไม่ค่อยถูกชะตากับเขา
- × **Bad response:** "It means 'I don't like him.'"
- ✓ **Good response:** "มันคือเวลาที่รู้สึกว่าไม่คลิกกับใครบางคน" (It's when you feel you don't click with someone.)

Try it with these:

- อยากกินของหวาน → ___________
- อากาศร้อนมากวันนี้ → ___________
- ลืมชื่อเธอไปแล้ว → ___________
- ไม่อยากออกไปคืนนี้ → ___________
- น่าจะได้นอนเยอะกว่านี้ → ___________

Pro Tip: Imagine explaining the phrase to someone who doesn't speak English!

Exercise #3: 'Think in Phrases' Challenge

Goal: Train your brain to **start Thai sentences without needing English first.**

Native speakers **don't construct sentences word by word**—they **use common phrase** patterns that **flow naturally**.

How the Drill Works:

1. Look at a Thai phrase starter.
2. Complete the sentence **entirely in Thai**, using your instincts.
3. Don't think in English first!

Example:

▷ **Thai:** คือว่า... (The thing is...)
× **Bad response:** *"I don't know how to say this."* (Thinking in English.)
✓ **Good response:** คือว่าวันนี้เหนื่อยมากเลย ("The thing is, today I'm really tired.")

Try it with these:

- ไม่แน่ใจว่า... **(Not sure if...)** → ___________
- รู้สึกว่า... **(Feels like...)** → ___________
- อยากจะบอกว่า... **(Want to say that...)** → ___________
- เอาจริง ๆ แล้ว... **(Honestly, actually...)** → ___________
- ถ้าทำได้... **(If I could...)** → ___________

Pro Tip: The more you practice **starting thoughts in Thai,** the easier it will be to **think in Thai automatically.**

7-Day Thai Thinking Challenge

Now that you've trained your brain with exercises, it's time to put them into action with **a full week of Thai thinking**.

How it works: Each day, you'll focus on **replacing English-based thinking** with **Thai-style thinking** in your daily routine.

- **Day 1: Describe Your Surroundings in Thai**
  Every time you walk into a new place, mentally describe it in Thai.
  Example: "ห้องนี้กว้างมากและมีหน้าต่างติดผ้าม่านสีแดง"

- **Day 2: Narrate Your Actions in Thai**
  As you go through your day, **think about what you're doing** in Thai.
  Example: "กำลังชงกาแฟ แล้วค่อยเริ่มทำงาน"

- **Day 3: Ask Yourself Questions in Thai**
  Throughout the day, **think in Thai questions** instead of English ones.
  Example: Instead of "What time is it?" → "ตอนนี้กี่โมงแล้ว?"

- **Day 4: Use Thai Fillers Instead of English**
  Whenever you pause in conversation, **use Thai fillers** instead of English ones.
  Example: Instead of "Uhm… I think…" → "เอ่อ... คิดว่า..."

- **Day 5: Think in Thai Verbs First**
  When forming a thought, **start with the verb** instead of the subject.
  Example: Instead of "I need to study" → **"ต้องอ่านหนังสือ"**

- **Day 6: Use a Thai Inner Monologue**
  For at least 10 minutes, **force yourself to think entirely in Thai.**
  Example: "หลังจากกินข้าว จะออกไปเดินเล่นสักหน่อย"

- **Day 7: Have a No-English Day**
  Challenge yourself to **go a full day thinking only in Thai**—no English allowed.
  Example: Every time you catch yourself thinking in English, **pause and switch to Thai.**

By now, your brain is **learning to structure thoughts like a Thai speaker**. Instead of thinking **in English and translating**, you're **starting thoughts naturally in Thai**.

Now that you've trained your **thought structure**, the next step is to **adopt a true Thai-speaker mentality**.

In the next chapter, we'll explore **how culture shapes language and thought—so you don't just sound fluent, but actually think like a native Thai speaker.**

CHAPTER FIVE:
Adopting a Thai Speaker's Mentality

THE TIME I ALMOST GOT ROBBED IN BANGKOK (BECAUSE OF AN IDIOM FAIL)

The first thing they tell you when you arrive in Bangkok is: **watch out for pickpockets**.

The second thing they don't tell you is: **watch out for your own Thai mistakes**—because they can get you into just as much trouble.

This is the story of how I learned both lessons the hard way.

It all started in the old town near Ratchadamnoen Avenue. I was feeling like a pro. My Thai was improving, I had been ordering pad kra pao without pointing at pictures, and I was starting to blend in—well, at least in my own mind.

That day, I was walking through the Chatuchak Market, a massive weekend bazaar known for vintage finds, street food, and the occasional suspicious electronics. I had read that you could negotiate for anything here. So, when I spotted a sleek, black leather bag that would've cost three times as much in a Bangkok mall, I decided to put my Thai skills to the ultimate test.

I approached the vendor, a short, leathery-skinned man with a gold ring and a cigarette permanently stuck to his lips.

- "ราคาเท่าไหร่ครับ?" I asked, casually.

- "พันห้าร้อย," he shot back.

I had done my homework—I knew bargaining was expected. So, I tried to negotiate like a local.

- "โอ้ย แพงจนถึงดาวเลย ไม่มีเงินนะพี่"
(Oh man, that's as expensive as the stars. I've got no money.)

He raised an eyebrow. That was my first mistake.

I should've said แพงมาก (super expensive), but instead, I threw in some phrase I vaguely remembered about things being "to the stars." I had no idea if that was even a real idiom in Thai, but hey, confidence is everything, right?

- "อืม..." he said, eyeing me up and down. "ไม่มีเงิน แล้วมีอะไร?"
(Hmm… no money? So what do you have?)

I panicked. I wanted to say, "I have nothing," but for some reason, my brain short-circuited, and I blurted out:

- "ผมหมดขาวแล้ว"
(Literally: "I'm out of white.")

Now, if I had been in Chiang Mai or just speaking to an innocent auntie at a temple, this might've passed as a bizarre but harmless phrase.

But here?

The vendor's expression changed. His gold ring glinted as he smirked. His cigarette dipped slightly.

- "หมดขาวเหรอ?" he said, nodding slowly, suddenly interested.

That's when I noticed something was off.

Two guys at a nearby stall turned their heads. A woman selling flip-flops gave me that Thai **look**—the subtle side glance that says, หนีไปตอนนี้เลย (Run. **Now.**)

Unbeknownst to me, in Bangkok street slang, ขาว (white) can sometimes refer to **certain illegal substances.**

So, in a single phrase, I had gone from broke tourist trying to haggle for a leather bag…

…to foreigner loudly announcing he was **out of drugs.**

The shift in energy was immediate. The vendor leaned closer, suddenly very eager to "help."

- "งั้นเดี๋ยวพี่จัดให้," he said, his tone dropping to a smooth whisper.
(Let me sort that out for you.)

Oh. No.

That's when I did **what any fluent-in-survival Thai speaker would do**.

I ran.

Straight into the labyrinth of market aisles, weaving past piles of sarongs, secondhand shoes, and rows of durian vendors. I turned one corner, then another, then another. Eventually, I lost them—but my heart was pounding when I ducked into a nearby iced tea stall and collapsed into a plastic chair.

The vendor looked over, raising an eyebrow.

- "เป็นอะไรหรือเปล่าครับ?"
(Are you okay?)

I wiped the sweat from my forehead.

- "จะซื้อกระเป๋า...แต่เกือบไปซื้อยาเข้าแทน"
(I tried to buy a bag… and almost bought drugs instead.)

He blinked. Then he laughed so hard he had to sit down.

And that's when I realized something crucial: **language isn't just words—it's culture.**

What makes perfect sense in one Thai-speaking region can mean something **completely different** in another.

And sometimes, if you mess it up…
…you'll end up accidentally offering to **buy drugs** at a Bangkok market.

The Big Lesson Here

At that moment, I realized that **Thai isn't just about grammar—it's about mentality.**

Thai speakers don't just think differently in terms of sentence structure. They **see the world differently**, and their language reflects that.

That's what this chapter is all about.

- How Thai distinguishes between what's **temporary and what's permanent**.
- Discover the secret behind Thai's 'to be' verbs and how understanding **temporary vs. permanent states** will transform your communication.
- Unpack the uniquely Thai mindset that separates fleeting feelings from lasting traits, and avoid common blunders that baffle native speakers.

By the end of this chapter, you won't just **speak** Thai better.

You'll **think like a Thai speaker.**

THE MINDSET BEHIND TEMPORARY VS. PERMANENT STATES IN THAI

Imagine you're at a bar in Bangkok, trying to blend in like a smooth, confident Thai speaker. The bartender asks how you're feeling, and you flash a grin and say:

- "ผมเป็นเหนื่อย."

He pauses. His eyebrows knit together.

You notice the slight shift in his expression—like you just said something… odd.

What went wrong? You meant to say, "I'm tired," but what you **actually** said was:

- **"I am permanently tired."**

As if exhaustion isn't just something happening to you **right now**, but a core, unchangeable fact about your existence.

The bartender, now mildly concerned for your well-being, offers you a seat and asks if everything is okay.

Why English Doesn't Have This Problem

The issue here comes down to a **fundamental difference in how Thai speakers think about being** compared to English speakers.

In English, we use "**to be**" for just about everything:

- ✓ *I am tired.*
- ✓ *I am happy.*
- ✓ *I am a teacher.*
- ✓ *I am in Bangkok.*

One verb. One job. No problem.

Thai, on the other hand, separates these ideas into more nuanced expressions—often avoiding "to be" altogether for feelings or conditions, and instead choosing verbs, adjectives, or contextual particles.

The result?

Thai has a built-in distinction between what's **temporary** and what's **permanent**.

So while English thinks of all these things as the same, Thai speakers see a major difference.

And if you mix them up, you might find yourself in some seriously awkward situations.

When "Permanent vs. Temporary" Goes Hilariously Wrong

Let's talk about some of the most common (and embarrassing) mix-ups that happen when English speakers don't understand this mindset shift.

1. "I Tried to Say Someone Was Being Silly... But Accidentally Called Them Permanently Stupid"

You're joking around with your Thai friends, and you want to say:

- *"You're being silly."*

But instead of saying ทำตัวตลก (You're acting silly), you say:

- เป็นคนโง่ *(You are a dumb person.)*

Congratulations, you've just insulted their intelligence on a **permanent level.** You didn't say they're joking—you said they are and always will be dumb.

Want to make it even worse? Try this:

- คุณโง่มากจริงๆ → Translation: "**You're seriously dumb.**"

Let's just say... **that friendship might not last much longer.**

2. "I Meant to Say 'I'm Bored'... But Instead, I Declared That I AM a Boring Person"

You're sitting in a long, drawn-out meeting and sigh:

- "ผมเป็นเบื่อ."

Your Thai coworker tilts their head.

Why? Because เป็นเบื่อ makes no sense in Thai. You've mashed together a being verb with an emotion that's already self-contained.

What you meant to say was:

✓ ผมเบื่อแล้ว. *(I'm bored now.)*

This shows a **temporary** emotional state, not your **permanent** personality.

Otherwise, you're saying you're the human version of a blank wall.

3. "That Time I Said a Friend Was Dead... Instead of Just Tired"

You're out with Thai friends and want to say:

- *"He's tired."*

But instead, you say:

- เขาเป็นเหนื่อย *(He is tiring.)*

Now, instead of showing empathy, you've just said your friend is the kind of person who exhausts everyone else.

And if you accidentally said เขาตายแล้ว thinking it was slang for **"he's dead tired,"** you might have just announced someone's actual death. In Thai, context matters. *A lot.*

The Mindset Shift: Thai Thinks in States, Not Just Labels

Here's what makes this grammar issue more than just grammar—it's a reflection of how Thai speakers perceive reality.

In English, we use "am" for everything.

In Thai, emotions and states don't need "to be"—they are already, and context decides the meaning.

Take a look at these:

English Thought	Thai Expression	Why It Matters
"I am happy."	ผมมีความสุข	Happiness is a **temporary** emotion.
"I am a happy person."	ผมเป็นคนมีความสุข	Your happiness is part of who you are.
"I am sick."	ผมไม่สบาย	You are sick **right now.**
"I am a sickly person."	ผมเป็นคนป่วยบ่อย	You have a **chronic condition.**
"I am in Bangkok."	ผมอยู่ที่กรุงเทพ	You are **currently** in Bangkok.
"Bangkok is in Thailand."	กรุงเทพอยู่ในประเทศไทย	Even locations use อยู่ because **nothing is forever.**

How to Train Your Brain to Think the Thai Way

Now that you **understand the mindset shift**, let's train your brain to stop making these mistakes.

1. Always ask yourself: Is this a temporary state or a permanent trait?

- ▷ If it's about **identity or long-term traits** → use เป็น (bpen).
- ▷ If it's about **where you are or how you feel right now** → use อยู่ (yùu) or just the adjective.

2. Picture two different scenarios:

- Imagine saying เป็นคนเบื่อ. Are you okay calling yourself permanently boring? If not, don't use เป็น.
- Imagine saying เขาเป็นตาย. That's not slang—it's a funeral announcement.

3. Practice with funny, real-world situations:

Convert these **English mistakes** into natural **Thai expressions:**

- "ผมเป็นเหนื่อย" *(I am permanently tired.)* → ____________
- "เขาเป็นโง่" *(He is permanently dumb.)* → ____________
- "ผมเป็นประหม่า" *(I am a nervous person.)* → ____________

HOW CULTURE SHAPES THE THAI LANGUAGE

If you've ever found yourself utterly confused by a Thai idiom, congratulations—you've just experienced **the cultural magic of language.**

Every language has expressions that don't translate well, but **Thai takes it to another level.** These aren't just phrases; they reveal **how Thai speakers think**—what they value, how they view time, relationships, and even how they insult each other.

And if you're not careful, misusing these expressions can lead to **some seriously hilarious misunderstandings**.

What Idioms Say About Culture

The Thai-speaking world has a distinct cultural mindset that seeps into everyday language.

Here's what you need to know:

- ✓ **Time is fluid.** There's a saying in Thai: เดี๋ยวก่อน (literally *"in a moment"*), but "a moment" could mean five minutes, five hours, or... **never**. Thai people tend to approach time with flexibility. It's not about rushing—it's about rhythm.

- ✓ **Family and social harmony matter.** Thai culture is more community-oriented than individualistic. That's why you hear expressions like บ้านของฉันก็คือบ้านของคุณ (*"My home is your home"*) and why elders, especially grandmothers (ยาย), often wield immense respect and influence in Thai families.

- ✓ **Politeness and indirectness are key.** Thai speakers avoid confrontation. Instead of saying "no" directly, someone might say เอาไว้ก่อนนะ (*"Let's wait and see"*), which usually means "not really," but with a soft, face-saving twist.

But the real fun begins when you try to use these idioms… and **completely butcher them.**

When Idioms Go Horribly Wrong

1. "I Tried to Say Someone Was Cheating... But Accidentally Said They Had a Buffalo Horn"

You're sitting in a café in Chiang Mai, and your Thai friend tells you about his breakup. You want to say something deep, something that shows you *get* it.

So, you remember a phrase you overheard and confidently say:

- "เขาใส่เขาให้เธอแล้วนะ"

Silence.

Your friend gives you a strange look.

What you meant to say was:

- ✓ *"He cheated on her."* (ใส่เขาให้ใครสักคน = **To cheat on someone)**

But what you imagined was:

- × *"He literally put a buffalo horn on her head."*

In your mind, you saw this poor woman walking through the market with giant horns. Because of course, that's what **"putting horns on someone"** sounds like… right?

Nope. In Thai, it's a symbolic way to describe infidelity. You've just learned the hard way that Thai idioms don't care about your literal translations.

2. "I Meant to Say Someone Was Spaced Out... But Accidentally Sent Them to Heaven"

Your coworker keeps zoning out in meetings. You want to say, **"You seem distracted."**

So, you think hard and say:

- "เหมือนคุณไปสวรรค์แล้วนะ"

Technically correct.

But in Thai, ไปสวรรค์ ("go to heaven") implies someone has died—not spaced out.

The better phrase?

✓ เหม่อลอยอยู่ (**“You’re spaced out”** or **“Your head is in the clouds.”**)

Now imagine telling an English speaker:

× *“You went to heaven.”*

…Yeah. Not exactly helpful.

Lesson learned: Thai idioms sound totally strange when translated word-for-word.

3. "I Wanted to Say Someone Was Blunt... But Instead, I Said They Had No Tongue Hair"

You’re talking about someone who’s **very straightforward** and doesn’t hold back.

In English, you’d say:

- *“He’s very direct.”*

But in Thai, the equivalent idiom is:

- พูดแบบไม่เกรงใจ *(“He speaks without holding back” or “He speaks without concern.”)*

Now imagine if you tried to be creative and said:

- เขาไม่มีขนลิ้น *(He has no hairs on his tongue.)*

...Your Thai friends would look very, very concerned.

Idioms just don’t play by logic. **They play by culture.**

The Cultural Mindset Behind These Expressions

Now that you've seen how idioms can go **hilariously wrong,** let's break down what they reveal about **Thai culture:**

Flexible Time:

- "เดี๋ยวนี้" *(Right now)* → Can mean now… or later.
- "รอสักครู่" *(Wait a moment)* → How long is a "moment"? No one really knows.

Strong Social Bonds:

- "น้ำพึ่งเรือ เสือพึ่งป่า" *(The water depends on the boat; the tiger depends on the forest)* → **Translation:** We all rely on each other.
- "ใกล้เกลือกินด่าง" *(Near the salt, but eat ashes)* → **Translation:** You overlook the good things that are close to you.

Emotional Nuance:

- "หมดแรง" *(Out of energy)* → To be completely drained.
- "ยกธงขาว" *(Raise the white flag)* → To give up.

Final Takeaway: How to Avoid Sounding Ridiculous

Now that you know **idioms are cultural reflections,** here's how to avoid **accidental disasters:**

- ✓ **Never translate idioms literally.** If you say *"You went to heaven"* in English, people will check if they missed a funeral.
- ✓ **Listen before you use them.** Thai speakers *know* when something sounds weird. If you're not 100% sure, ask first!
- ✓ **If you mess up… laugh it off!** Thai people appreciate effort. Just smile, laugh, and say พูดผิดเฉยๆ (*"Just a language fail"*) to show you're learning.

Now that you've **survived the idioms,** let's take things to the next level. In the next chapter, we'll dive into **how emotions, humor, and even flirting sound completely different in Thai**—so you can avoid any *romantic misunderstandings.*

CHAPTER SIX:
Vocabulary Without Translation

THE TIME I BUTCHERED A COMPLIMENT ON A DATE

She walked in, and my brain stopped working.

I mean, it just **shut down.**

You ever see someone so **unbelievably stunning** that you start questioning reality? Like, maybe you've been living your whole life in **black and white,** and suddenly—BAM—you're in full color, 4K Ultra HD?

That was **Pim.**

We were in Bangkok, at a rooftop bar near the Chao Phraya River that overlooked the city skyline. The sun had just dipped below the horizon, painting the sky in streaks of **pink, orange, and deep purple.** Candlelight flickered between us, casting shadows on her perfect cheekbones.

I had been **preparing for this moment.** I knew exactly what to say in Thai.

Or so I thought.

I wanted to compliment her dress. **Simple, right?** I was going to say:

- **"ชุดนี้สวยมากเลย"** (That dress is so beautiful.)

That's what I thought I said.

But instead, my brain—still malfunctioning from her sheer **beauty overload**—decided to mash together **random** Thai words like a chaotic AI generator.

I confidently smiled and said:

- "คุณคือชุดที่ร้อนมาก"

A pause.

Pim blinked. **Twice.**

Then she burst out **laughing**—but not in a cute, flirty way. No. This was full **cackling,** like I had just done the linguistic equivalent of tripping on my own shoelaces and falling face-first into a plate of tapas.

I had **no idea** what was so funny, but my confidence was already **free-falling off this rooftop.**

She wiped a tear from her eye and leaned forward. *"Did you just call me a... 'very hot outfit?'"*

Oh no.

Oh no, no, no.

I replayed my words in my head. My **fatal mistake** hit me like a truck.

- I meant to say "ชุดนี้สวยมากเลย" (That dress is beautiful.)
- Instead, I said "คุณคือชุดที่ร้อนมาก" (You are a very hot dress.)

I had **transformed this goddess of a woman into a sentient piece of overheated clothing.**

I wanted to launch myself **off the rooftop immediately.**

But instead of making my escape, I just did what any **reasonable person** would do in this situation.

I doubled down.

"Well," I stammered, scrambling to recover, "I mean… if anyone could be a dress, you'd be… the most fashionable one in all of Thailand."

Silence.

Pim smirked. *"So you think I am… a hot piece of fabric?"*

I stared at her, wide-eyed. I was **losing this battle** and sinking further into **linguistic doom.**

Then she did something unexpected.

She raised her glass, **clinked it against mine,** and said, *"I'll take it. A very hot dress it is."*

We both **laughed,** the tension broke, and somehow—**somehow**—the date wasn't ruined.

Big Lesson Here

That night, I learned something **critical** about learning vocabulary in Thai.

I had been **translating words in my head,** not **thinking in Thai.** My brain saw "hot" and defaulted to **ร้อน (rón),** even though that's not how you compliment someone in Thai.

The truth is, **you don't learn words by translating.** You learn them by **feeling them, associating them, and using them naturally.**

And that's exactly what this chapter is about.

THINKING IN IMAGES, NOT WORDS

Imagine this: You're in Thailand, trying to ask a waiter for a tissue. You confidently walk up to the waiter and say, **"ขอแผนที่หน่อยครับ/ค่ะ"**

The waiter stares at you, confused.

You notice his eyebrows furrow.

Wait… what did you just say?

Then it hits you: **You just asked for a map instead of a napkin.**

Not ideal when you've got mango sticky rice all over your fingers.

This is what happens when you learn words by direct translation instead of learning them the way native speakers do—**through images, context, and real-world experience.**

Why Direct Translation Slows You Down

Think about how you learned your first language.

Did your parents sit you down and explain, "Okay, the word 'apple' means a round, red fruit that grows on trees"?

Of course not.

Instead, they probably pointed at an apple, handed you one, and said, **"Apple."**

Your brain linked the **word** to the **object** itself—not to a word in another language.

But when learning Thai, most people make the mistake of trying to connect **Thai words to English words first** instead of connecting **Thai words directly to what they represent.**

That's why learners get stuck translating in their heads.

If you learn **พระอาทิตย์ขึ้น** (sunrise) by linking it to the English word "sunrise," every time you hear **พระอาทิตย์ขึ้น,** your brain will do this:

พระอาทิตย์ขึ้น → **"sunrise" → mental image of a sunrise.**

That's two unnecessary steps.

A native speaker just goes:

พระอาทิตย์ขึ้น → **mental image of a sunrise.**

If you **train yourself to associate words directly with images,** you'll start thinking in Thai instead of constantly translating.

How the Brain Processes Language Visually

Your brain **loves** images.

In fact, studies show that **people remember pictures far better than words** (this is called the **Picture Superiority Effect**).

That's why you can recall a movie scene from ten years ago but struggle to remember what you had for breakfast last Tuesday.

So if you train your brain to connect Thai words to **images, emotions, and real-world experiences,** instead of English translations, you'll **learn faster and remember better.**

The Comedy of Direct Translation Fails

Let's be honest—bad translations are hilarious.

Here are some **real-life** examples of how translation mistakes can go *horribly* wrong:

1. The Pregnant Tourist

A classic mistake: Thinking **"อาย"** (shy or embarrassed) sounds like **"ท้อง"** (pregnant).

So when you try to say **"I'm embarrassed"**, you confidently declare:

- **"ฉันท้องค่ะ"** (I'm pregnant.)

And now your polite apology sounds like a life announcement.

2. The Very Hot Guy

Let's say you're in Bangkok, and you see an **attractive** guy.

You want to say: **"Wow, he's hot."**

But instead of saying “เขาหล่อมาก” (He’s handsome), you blurt out:

- “เขาร้อนมาก” (He is very hot—as in, overheating.)

Yeah, that’s going to get some *looks.*

3. The Rice Disaster

You’re at a Thai friend’s house and want to compliment the rice.

You say:

- “ข้าวอร่อยตลอด” (Rice is always delicious.)

Which… technically makes sense, but sounds robotic.

Better would be:

- “ข้าววันนี้อร่อยมากเลย” (The rice today is really delicious.)

In Thai, context matters—and generalizing everything doesn’t always land right.

How to Use Visualization to Learn Thai Words Faster

Now that you know **why** direct translation is a bad idea, let’s go over **how to train your brain** to think in images instead of words.

1. Picture It Instead of Translating It

Instead of memorizing a word like พระอาทิตย์ขึ้น by translating it to "sunrise," close your eyes and **visualize**:

- The soft glow of the early morning sun.
- A street in Chiang Mai just as morning vendors open their stalls.
- The sound of a rooster crowing as the sun crests over rice fields.

Now, every time you hear พระอาทิตย์ขึ้น, your brain **goes straight to the image**—no English needed.

2. Act It Out

Ever notice how you remember song lyrics better than a random list of words?

That's because **your body and emotions help you learn.**

Try **acting out** words while saying them in Thai:

- กระโดด (to jump) → Actually jump.
- วิ่ง (to run) → Jog in place.
- นอนหลับ (to sleep) → Pretend to snore.

The more **movement and emotion** you involve, the better you remember.

3. Use Image Flashcards (Not Word Flashcards)

Instead of writing "**หมา = Dog**" on a flashcard, find a picture of a dog and write "**หมา**" under it.

That way, you **connect the word to the image**—not to an English translation.

4. Learn Words in Context, Not Isolation

It's easier to remember words **in full sentences** instead of in isolation.

For example:

Instead of memorizing **"โต๊ะ" (table)**, try:

- "ฉันจะวางอาหารบนโต๊ะ"
  (I'm going to put the food on the table.)

Now you **see** a table with food on it. You're not just memorizing the word—you're experiencing it.

Practice Exercise: Describe Without Translating

Look around you. **Pick three objects.**

Now, describe them **entirely in Thai**—without thinking of the English words first.

Example:

- Instead of: **"The lamp is bright."** (thinking in English first)
- Try: **"โคมไฟสว่างมากเลย"** (directly in Thai)

Do this **daily,** and before you know it, you'll start thinking in Thai naturally. But what good is learning words if they slip away just as fast? Let's make them stick for good with some powerful memory hacks.

THE POWER OF CONTEXT IN LEARNING NEW WORDS

Let's play a quick game.

Imagine you're in Thailand, walking through a lively market in Chiang Mai. You hear a group of locals crowded around a tiny noodle stall, watching a football match on a small TV.

Suddenly, they all cheer and yell,

- "ยิงเข้าแล้วโว้ย!"

You have no idea what it means.

But from their reactions—the clapping, the excitement, the screen showing a slow-motion replay of a goal—you **instinctively understand:**

It must be something good. Something **big.**

That's how powerful **context** is.

You don't need a dictionary. You don't need to stop and translate. You just **get it**—because your brain is wired to learn language through real-world situations, not isolated words.

And that's exactly how you should be learning Thai.

Why Memorizing Lists Doesn't Work

Think about how most people try to learn vocabulary.

They sit down, open a book, and memorize a list like this:

- โต๊ะ – Table
- กระจก – Mirror
- โคมไฟ – Lamp
- เตา – Stove

The problem?

There's **no context.** No **real-world connection.** Just a boring list of words that your brain has zero reason to remember.

Compare that to how you naturally learn new words in your native language:

- You learn โต๊ะ because someone tells you, "วางจานบนโต๊ะสิ" (Put your plate on the table.)
- You learn โคมไฟ because someone says, "เปิดโคมไฟหน่อย มันมืดแล้ว" (Turn on the lamp, it's dark.)

You're **experiencing** the words, not just memorizing them.

That's why **learning words in context** is the fastest way to expand your vocabulary.

How Words Gain Meaning from Situations

Context doesn't just help you **learn** new words—it also stops you from making embarrassing mistakes.

Let's look at some words that completely change depending on how they're used:

1. "แรงมาก!" – Wait... Are They Talking About Strength?

You might think it means someone is physically strong.

But if you're in Bangkok and your friend tells you:

- "เมื่อวานแฟนเก่าฉันไปคอมเมนต์ด่าฉันในเฟซบุ๊กต่อหน้าแฟนใหม่!" (My ex commented something nasty about me on Facebook… right in front of my new partner!)

Their friend might react:

- "แรงมาก!" (Savage!)

And if you respond with:

- "อ๋อ เขาออกกำลังกายเยอะเหรอ?" (Oh, they work out a lot?)

…you've completely missed the point.

2. "ไม่เป็นไร" – It's Not Just "Nothing's Wrong"

If you directly translate "ไม่เป็นไร" you get:

× **"It's nothing."**

But Thai people use it in so many ways:

✓ **"Don't worry about it."**
✓ **"It's okay."**
✓ **"No problem."**
✓ **"I forgive you."**
✓ **"You don't owe me anything."**

So if you spill iced tea on someone's bag and they say "ไม่เป็นไร", they're not saying nothing happened.

They're saying:

- **"It's okay. Chill."**

3. "ตั้งใจหน่อยสิ" – Focus, Not Fix!

If your Thai teacher says:

- "ถ้าอยากพูดเก่ง ต้องตั้งใจหน่อยสิ"

You might hear: "ตั้งใจ = **Fix?**"

Nope.

What they're really saying is:

- **"Pay attention. Focus more."**

Not "repair" anything.

Phrases don't always mean what they literally say—and that's where **context saves you.**

How to Use Thai Media to Absorb New Words

Now that you know why **context is everything,** let's look at some **practical ways** to start learning Thai this way—without memorizing boring word lists.

1. Watch TV Shows & Guess New Words

Instead of looking up every single word, **train your brain to guess meanings from context.**

- ▷ **Step 1:** Pick a Thai show (with or without subtitles).
- ▷ **Step 2:** Listen for words you don't know.
- ▷ **Step 3:** Guess their meaning based on tone, facial expressions, and situation.
- ▷ **Step 4:** Look up the word AFTER you've made your guess.

Example: Watching a Thai soap opera, you hear:

- "อย่ามาทำแบบนี้กับฉันอีกนะ!"

Even without knowing the words, you feel the emotion.

You can probably guess:

- **"Don't do that to me again!"**

Once you confirm it, you'll never forget it—because you learned it **naturally.**

2. Use Music to Pick Up Phrases

Thai songs are **goldmines** for real, natural expressions.

- ▹ **Step 1:** Choose a Thai song.
- ▹ **Step 2:** Listen closely to a phrase that repeats.
- ▹ **Step 3:** Guess what it means based on emotion and melody.

Example: In the song "แพ้ใจ" **(Paé Jai)**, you hear:

- "ยอมแพ้ทั้งๆ ที่ใจยังรักเธออยู่"

Even if you don't understand every word, you feel the heartbreak.

Later, you learn it means:

- **"I gave up… even though my heart still loves you."**

Now those words are linked to music, emotion—and you'll *own* them forever.

3. The "Guess First" Exercise

- **Step 1:** Watch a **Thai video** (YouTube, Netflix, TikTok).
- **Step 2:** Write down **5 words** you don't know.
- **Step 3: Guess their meaning** based on context.
- **Step 4: Check if you were right.**

Example: Watching a cooking video, you hear:

- "พอผัดเสร็จแล้วก็ใส่ไข่ลงไปเลยนะ"

You don't know **"ผัด" (phàt)**. But you see them stirring vegetables in a pan.

Your guess? **"Stir-fry."**

Nailed it. Now **"ผัด = stir-fry"** is stored deep in your long-term memory.

MEMORY HACKS FOR LOCKING IN NEW WORDS

Imagine you're on a first date. The chemistry is electric. The conversation is flowing. And then—disaster.

You're trying to impress your date with your Thai skills, but instead of saying "ชอบเสียงหัวเราะของคุณ" (I love your laugh), you confidently blurt out:

- "ชอบข้าวของคุณ"
  (Translation: I love your rice.)

Your date stares at you. The romantic moment is **dead.**

That's what happens when words don't stick in your brain the right way.

But what if I told you that **you'll never forget the word "laugh" again?** Because now, every time you think of laughing in Thai, you'll remember **that date where you accidentally declared your love for rice.**

Welcome to the world of memory hacks.

Memorizing new words **doesn't have to be boring.** In fact, the more ridiculous, emotional, or personal the connection, the **faster** your brain locks it in.

Here's how to **hack your memory** so that Thai words **never slip away again.**

The Science of Memory: Why You Forget & How to Stop It

Ever wonder why you can remember **embarrassing moments from 10 years ago**, but forget a Thai word you learned **10 minutes ago?**

That's because your brain **prioritizes emotional, funny, and strange things.**

Boring information? **Gone in seconds.**
Something ridiculous? **Burned into your memory forever.**

Let's test this:

Which of these is easier to remember?

1. **Key = กุญแจ**
2. **"Imagine a giant goon (กุญ) with jazz hands (แจ) unlocking your fridge and dancing inside."**

The second one is **way** stickier because your brain thrives on **bizarre and visual** connections.

So instead of cramming words like a robot, **let's hack your memory with weird, emotional, and fun techniques.**

Word Association: Connect Words to Personal Experiences

Let's say you struggle to remember **"แพง" (expensive).**

A boring way to learn it:

× Repeating **"แพง means expensive"** 20 times.

A **better** way to learn it:

✓ **"Bangkok shopping is a PAIN (แพง) for my wallet."**

The trick? **Linking the word to something personal.**

Here are more examples:

- **ร้อน (hot)** → Imagine the sun roasting your forehead in April heat = "Ron is roasting me."
- **แครอท (carrot)** → Picture a carrot doing karaoke. "Carrot-karaoke = แครอท."
- **ผม (hair)** → Picture your friend Pom always fixing his hair. Pom = ผม = hair.

Exercise: Pick five tricky words and create a personal link for each.

The Storytelling Method: Make Your Brain Work For You

Your brain loves **stories.**

Let's try a classic **story memory trick:**

Say you need to remember these five words:

1. แมว (cat)
2. กุญแจ (key)
3. กระจก (mirror)
4. รองเท้า (shoes)
5. ประตู (door)

Instead of memorizing them **individually**, we turn them into a **weird, unforgettable story:**

One night, your CAT (แมว) steals your golden KEY (กุญแจ) and jumps through a magical MIRROR (กระจก). You chase after it but trip over your SINGING SHOES (รองเท้า), which yell at you to open the DOOR (ประตู) before the cat escapes into another dimension.

Now you're not memorizing—**you're watching a movie in your head.**

Exercise: Take 5 Thai words and create a short, ridiculous story with them.

Mnemonics & Rhyming Tricks: The Musical Brain Hack

Have you ever heard a song once and **accidentally memorized the lyrics?**

That's because rhymes and rhythm **boost memory retention by 80%.**

Now, let's use **rhymes to hack Thai words into your brain:**

- เนื้อ (meat) = "Eat MEAT with NEUA sauce."
- เร็ว (fast) = "Run real fast like a Thai RAIL."
- ทำงาน (work) = "TUM my job, NAAN I'm tired."

Even better? Make it **musical**:

- "ท้องฟ้าเป็นสีฟ้า, หัวใจก็เหมือนกัน" **(Sky is blue, my heart is too.)** → ฟ้า = sky
- "เงิน เงิน มันไม่พอ ใช่ไหมล่ะพี่บัวขา" **(Money, money, never enough.)** → เงิน = money

Now, instead of *memorizing*, you're *singing Thai into your brain.*

Exercise: Create three rhymes for tricky Thai words.

CHAPTER SEVEN:

The Immersion Mindset (Without Leaving Home)

THE TIME I GOT LOST ON A MOUNTAIN IN CHIANG MAI (AND HOW IT CHANGED MY THAI FOREVER)

It started as **just another YouTube video idea for my YouTube channel**—a scenic hike up a mountain in **northern Thailand,** capturing breathtaking views, local wildlife, and maybe throwing in some Thai practice for good measure.

At least, that's how it *started.*

What actually happened? **I almost disappeared into the jungle forever.**

Let me explain.

I was in Chiang Mai, Thailand, and after hearing about a "relaxing" hike up Doi Suthep from some locals at a small coffee stand, I figured it would be the perfect **YouTube adventure**. Great scenery, some Thai conversations along the way, and, if I was lucky, **a few viral-worthy moments.**

I packed my camera, a bottle of water, and **way too much confidence.**

Then I hit the trail.

About 30 minutes in, I ran into a friendly **older Thai man** coming down the trail. He was **all smiles**, and we started chatting in Thai.

Him: "ไปคนเดียวเหรอ?"
(Are you going alone?)

Me: "ใช่ครับ อากาศดี เดินเล่นหน่อย"
(Yeah, the weather's nice. Just going for a walk.)

He gave me a look—like **a mix of concern and amusement**—then said something **fast**.

Really fast.

I only caught bits and pieces:

"ไม่มีคน... ลื่น... ข้างหน้า... อันตราย..."

Something about **danger** and... **slipping?**

But instead of *asking for clarification,* I just nodded, smiled, and hit him with the classic clueless response**:**

"อ๋อๆ ไม่มีปัญหา!"
(Ohh yeah, no problem!)

Spoiler alert: There was, in fact, a problem.

An hour later, I was **high up the mountain, completely alone,** and the trail was getting **steeper, muddier, and more questionable** by the minute.

And then—I saw it.

The sign.

Hand-painted, barely legible, on a piece of rotting wood tied to a tree:

"อันตราย ห้ามเข้า"
(DANGER. DO NOT ENTER.)

At this point, any *sensible person* would have turned around.

But what did I do?

I did what **every confident, slightly overambitious YouTuber** does when faced with danger:

I kept going.

Because **content.**

I climbed over the sign, camera in hand, and **immediately regretted everything.**

Less than **ten minutes later,** the trail *vanished.*

Gone.

Just mud, thick trees, and way too many creepy noises around me.

Then I remembered what the **old man** had said earlier.

"ไม่มีคน... ลื่น... ข้างหน้า... อันตราย..."

Translation:

"No people… slippery… ahead… dangerous…"

Ah.

There I was—**on a slippery slope, deep in the Thai jungle, alone.**

Fantastic.

Then I heard **something rustling** in the trees behind me.

And that was it—**my fluency in Thai suddenly reached peak survival mode.**

I started **talking to myself** out loud, trying to think through the situation in Thai:

“โอเค... ใจเย็นก่อน... หาทางกลับให้เจอ...”
(Okay… calm down… find the way back…)

I turned around.

“ฟังสิ... หรือมีใครอยู่แถวนี้...”
(Listen… maybe someone’s nearby…)

Nope.

Nothing but jungle.

Then I did what any **logical** person would do in this situation:

I started **yelling in Thai.**

“สวัสดีครับ! มีใครอยู่ไหม?!”
(Hello! Is anyone there?!)

Nothing.

Just **more rustling.**

My brain went into **full panic mode.** I had two options:

1. **Accept my fate and become the first foreign YouTuber to go missing in the Thai wilderness.**
2. **Figure out how the hell to get back—fast.**

Guess which one I picked?

Long story short: **After 20 minutes of blind panic, I retraced my steps and found the real trail again.**

I got back **muddy, exhausted, and questioning my life choices.**

But here's the weird part:

That was the first time I had spent **a full hour thinking entirely in Thai.**

No English translations. No hesitation. Just **pure Thai survival mode.**

That moment **changed everything** for me.

It made me realize that the **fastest way to immerse yourself in Thai isn't in a classroom or an app**—it's by creating an environment where **English isn't an option.**

Lucky for you, you don't need to risk your life in the Thai jungle to make it happen.

So in this chapter, I'm going to show you how to **build that same immersion mindset from home**—from the safety of your home.

Let's go!

THE 24-HOUR THAI CHALLENGE

Imagine waking up tomorrow morning and deciding that, for the next **24 hours,** you are not allowed to use **a single word of English.** No English thoughts, no English texts, no English TV, no English anything.

Could you do it?

It sounds simple in theory. But in practice?

Welcome to the **ultimate immersion experiment.** This is the **24-Hour Thai Challenge,** and if you complete it, you'll unlock a level of fluency training that most Thai learners never experience.

Why 24 Hours of Thai-Only Will Change Your Brain

Your brain is **lazy.** It likes shortcuts. That's why, even if you're learning Thai, it still defaults to English in your thoughts, speech, and habits.

But what if we didn't give it a choice?

This challenge forces your brain to adapt. When you're hungry, you can't just think, *I need food.* You have to think, หิวข้าว. When you're texting your friend, you can't write, *I'll be there in 10 minutes.* You have to say, ถึงในสิบนาที.

The first few hours feel like trying to run in knee-deep water. But by the end of the day?

Your brain starts to switch into Thai mode—naturally.

Step 1: Preparing for the Challenge

Like any great adventure, you need a plan. Here's what you should do **before** your 24-hour immersion day starts:

- ✓ **Change your phone settings to Thai.** (Yes, including Siri/ Google Assistant.)
- ✓ **Set up Thai-only media.** (YouTube, Netflix, Thai music playlists, audiobooks, podcasts.)
- ✓ **Tell your friends and family.** (So they don't freak out when you only text them in Thai.)
- ✓ **Prepare a "cheat sheet" of essential phrases.** (If you suddenly forget how to say, I need to go to the bathroom, you don't want to panic.)
- ✓ **Make a plan for Thai interactions.** (Will you go to a local Thai food stall? Chat online with a Thai tutor?)

Now that your Thai world is set up, let's begin.

Step 2: Your 24-Hour Thai Schedule

Here's how your day of **no-English survival** will go:

Morning: Thai Mindset Activation

- ▹ **Wake up.** Before you even get out of bed, think: วันนี้วันอะไร? จะทำอะไรดีนะ?
- ▹ **Journal in Thai.** Write a simple **morning reflection** (even if it's just ง่วงนอนมาก อยากกินกาแฟ)
- ▹ **Make breakfast while narrating your actions.** กำลังต้มไข่ เดี๋ยวชงกาแฟ แล้วก็ปิ้งขนมปัง
- ▹ **Listen to a Thai podcast or music as you eat.**

The goal: Start the day with **zero English thoughts.**

Afternoon: Real-World Thai Immersion

- ▹ **Watch a Thai YouTube video or TV show.** No subtitles. No pausing. Just absorb.
- ▹ **Text friends only in Thai.** (Or post something simple on social media in Thai.)
- ▹ **Order food in Thai.** If you're at a restaurant, try speaking with the waiter. If you're at home, use a Thai cooking tutorial.
- ▹ **Talk to yourself out loud in Thai.** Pretend you're vlogging your day: ตอนนี้อยู่ที่ตลาด เดี๋ยวจะซื้อผลไม้กับข้าวเหนียวหมูปิ้ง

The goal: Live your life normally—just in Thai.

Evening: Reflection & Reinforcement

- ▹ **Read in Thai.** A book, an article, or even just Thai tweets.
- ▹ **Watch a Thai movie.** Again, no English subtitles allowed!
- ▹ **Write a summary of your day in Thai.** What was hard? What words did you struggle with?
- ▹ **Record a voice memo in Thai.** Talk about your day, your thoughts, or what you learned.

The goal: Finish the day having **thought, spoken, written, and lived in Thai.**

Step 3: What You'll Learn from This Challenge

By the end of the day, you will realize three things:

1. **You know more Thai than you thought.**
2. **Your brain starts thinking in Thai naturally when it has no choice.**
3. **You will make mistakes. Many. And that's good.**

The first time I did this challenge, I accidentally told a vendor: ผมร้อนแรงมาก instead of ผมรู้สึกร้อน. Which doesn't mean I'm hot (because of the weather)—it means something more like **I'm feeling... passionately fiery.**

Lesson learned.

And that's the point! This challenge **forces mistakes,** and mistakes make you learn **faster** than any textbook ever will.

Final Thought: Are You Ready to Try?

If you complete this challenge, even just once, you will **notice an immediate shift** in how you think and process Thai.

You don't have to do it perfectly. You just have to do it.

And who knows? Maybe one day, **your brain will just wake up thinking in Thai—without even trying.**

CREATING A THAI BUBBLE IN YOUR DAILY LIFE

You've probably heard that to become fluent, you need to "immerse yourself" in Thai. But what does that actually mean if you're not living in Thailand? Do you need to buy a plane ticket and move to Bangkok or Chiang Mai? Nope.

The key to fluency isn't just about studying Thai—it's about surrounding yourself with it **every single day.** You want to create a "Thai Bubble"—an environment where Thai is your default, not English.

Passive vs. Active Immersion: The Fluency Formula

Most learners **only** do passive immersion. They listen to Thai music, watch Netflix in Thai, and maybe follow a Thai-speaking influencer or two.

But that's not enough.

If you're only **consuming** Thai without actually **producing** it, your fluency will be stuck in first gear.

Here's the golden rule:

- ✓ **Passive immersion = Exposure.** (Listening, reading, watching Thai content.)
- ✓ **Active immersion = Practice.** (Speaking, writing, thinking in Thai.)

Both are necessary, but **active immersion is where real fluency happens.**

Let's build your Thai Bubble with **both** types of immersion so your brain starts functioning in Thai **automatically**.

Step 1: Replacing English with Thai in Your Daily Habits

Want to start thinking in Thai? Then **flood your environment** with it. Here's how:

1. Change Your Phone & App Settings to Thai

Your phone is your most-used device—why is it still in English?

- ✓ Go to **Settings → Language & Region → Switch to Thai**
- ✓ Change your apps to Thai: Instagram, TikTok, Netflix, YouTube—everything.
- ✓ Voice assistants? Set Siri or Google Assistant to Thai.

You'll learn **real, useful words** just by using your phone—without even thinking about it.

2. Follow Thai-Speaking Creators on Social Media

Your Instagram and TikTok feeds are **mind-control devices**—so why not make them work in your favor?

- ✓ **Follow Thai-speaking influencers, comedians, and YouTubers.**
- ✓ **Unfollow or mute English-speaking content for a while.** (Seriously.)
- ✓ **Engage! Comment on Thai posts, reply to stories in Thai—practice!**

If you scroll every day, you might as well be absorbing Thai while doing it.

3. Make Thai the Soundtrack of Your Life

Fluency isn't just about studying—it's about **making Thai the background noise of your life.**

- ✓ **Listen to Thai podcasts** while driving, cooking, or working out.
- ✓ **Play Thai music** while showering, doing laundry, or walking.
- ✓ **Watch Thai TV, movies, and YouTube videos daily.**

Even if you don't understand everything, your brain is **absorbing** the rhythm, sounds, and patterns of Thai.

4. Write Your Daily Life in Thai

- ✓ **To-do lists:** Write your tasks for the day in Thai.
- ✓ **Reminders & alarms:** Set them in Thai.
- ✓ **Text yourself in Thai:** Use WhatsApp or Notes to practice writing.

Your goal? **Make Thai the language of your thoughts and actions.**

Step 2: "Micro-Immersion" Techniques

Big immersion trips are great—but **small daily habits** will get you further than a month in Thailand ever could. Try these:

1. Talk to Yourself in Thai Throughout the Day

Yes, talk to yourself. Out loud.

- ✓ Narrate what you're doing: "กำลังชงกาแฟ แล้วค่อยทำงานต่อนะ" (Making coffee, then I'll continue working.)
- ✓ Ask yourself questions: "เอ๊ะ...วางกุญแจไว้ที่ไหนนะ?" (Where did I put the keys?)
- ✓ Think in Thai instead of English whenever possible.

2. Create a "Thai-Only" Zone in Your Home

Pick a spot—your bedroom, your kitchen, your car—and declare it an **English-free zone.**

- ✓ **Only listen, read, and speak in Thai** when you're in that space.
- ✓ **Put Thai books, labels, or sticky notes** to reinforce the habit.
- ✓ **If you live with someone, tell them they can only speak Thai with you in that area.**

3. Label Everything in Thai

If you see it, **you should know its name in Thai.**

- ✓ **Grab sticky notes and start labeling:** ประตู (door), กระจก (mirror), โต๊ะ (table).
- ✓ **Every time you see an object, say the word in Thai in your head.**
- ✓ **Swap out old labels as you master them.**

Your home should feel like a **Thai classroom—without the boring grammar drills.**

The Unexpected Side Effects of Living in Thai

When you truly immerse yourself, **Thai takes over your brain.** Here's what happens:

- **You start answering in Thai without thinking.** *("ขอบคุณครับ" to an English-speaking cashier... Oops!)*
- **You start forgetting the English word for things.** *(What's the word for แก้วน้ำ again? Oh... glass.)*
- **You dream in Thai.** *(That's when you know you're winning.)*

Immersion rewires your brain. The more you surround yourself with Thai, the **faster fluency comes.**

Your 7-Day "Thai Bubble" Challenge

If you're serious about immersion, here's your challenge: **Create a Thai-only week.**

- **Day 1:** Change your phone and apps to Thai.
- **Day 2:** Only follow Thai-speaking content on social media.
- **Day 3:** Write all your daily lists, notes, and reminders in Thai.
- **Day 4:** Watch a Thai movie or show with subtitles in Thai.
- **Day 5:** Narrate your daily routine out loud in Thai.
- **Day 6:** Label everything in your house with Thai words.
- **Day 7:** Have a full "Thai-Only" Day—no English allowed!

By the end of this challenge, Thai will no longer feel like a foreign language—it will be a part of your life.

But what if you don't have anyone to practice speaking with? That's what we'll tackle next.

THE SECRET TO SPEAKING MORE (EVEN WHEN YOU'RE ALONE)

One of the biggest hurdles for Thai learners isn't just learning vocabulary or grammar—it's **speaking confidently.** And yet, most people don't get enough speaking practice because they feel like they need a native speaker to talk to. **But what if I told you that you don't need anyone else to improve your speaking skills?**

This section is all about training yourself to **speak Thai fluently, even when you're completely alone.** By the end, you'll have practical strategies to **build confidence, improve pronunciation, and develop conversational reflexes**—all without relying on a speaking partner.

Why Speaking Is Non-Negotiable for Fluency

A common mistake language learners make is focusing too much on input—**listening and reading**—without balancing it with **output—speaking and writing.**

Think about it: If you want to get good at basketball, you can't just watch NBA games all day. You have to pick up a ball and **shoot some hoops.**

It's the same with Thai.

If you're only listening to podcasts or watching Netflix in Thai but never actually speaking, **your brain isn't training itself to produce the language in real time.** This is why people say, "I can understand Thai, but I can't speak it."

That changes **right now.**

How to Practice Speaking Without a Partner

1. The Talk to Yourself Method

It might feel strange at first, **but talking to yourself in Thai is one of the fastest ways to improve fluency.** Native speakers don't just think in words; they **verbalize thoughts effortlessly.** You need to train your brain to do the same.

How to do it:

- Narrate your actions throughout the day: **"กำลังจะชงกาแฟ ขอใช้แก้วโปรดหน่อยนะ"** (I'm going to make coffee. Let me grab my favorite mug.)
- Describe what you see: **"ท้องฟ้ามืดครึ้มวันนี้ ดูเหมือนฝนจะตกแน่ๆ"** (The sky is cloudy today. Looks like it's going to rain.)
- Have pretend conversations: Ask yourself questions and answer them as if you're talking to a friend.

Bonus Challenge:

Every night, **recap your day in Thai.** Just talk about what you did, what you ate, or what surprised you. This reinforces past-tense usage and builds fluency.

2. The Voice Memo Method

Want to **track your progress** and build confidence? Start recording yourself speaking Thai. It's like journaling—but out loud.

How to do it:

- Pick a topic (your weekend plans, a story from your day, a random Thai prompt).
- Speak for **one to two minutes without stopping.**
- Listen to your recording and note mistakes or awkward pauses.
- Repeat the process the next day and try to improve!

Why this works:

- It forces you to **think on your feet.**
- You become **aware of pronunciation mistakes.**
- You can **track improvement** over time.

3. Roleplaying Conversations

Even if you don't have a native speaker around, you can **simulate real conversations.** This makes you more comfortable for when you actually interact with others.

Try these roleplay exercises:

✓ **Ordering food:** Pretend you're at a Thai street food stall and practice ordering. "ขอข้าวผัดหมูหนึ่งจาน กับน้ำเปล่าแก้วนึง ครับ/ค่ะ" (I'd like one plate of pork fried rice and a glass of water, please.)

- ✓ **Meeting someone new:** Introduce yourself and talk about your interests. "สวัสดีครับ/ค่ะ ผม/ฉันชื่อ [your name] มาจาก [your country] ชอบท่องเที่ยวมากเลยครับ/ค่ะ" (Hi, my name is [your name]. I'm from [your country] and I love traveling.)
- ✓ **Handling an everyday situation:** Imagine booking a hotel room or asking for directions. "ขอโทษครับ/ค่ะ ช่วยบอกทางไปสถานีรถไฟได้ไหมครับ/ค่ะ?" (Excuse me, could you tell me how to get to the train station?)

If you want **extra practice,** you can use AI tools like ChatGPT to simulate a Thai conversation.

Final Takeaway: Speak More, Fear Less

The key to fluency isn't **perfect grammar or a huge vocabulary**—it's the ability to speak without overthinking. And the **only way to get there is by speaking more.**

Here's your challenge:

1. Talk to yourself in Thai for **five minutes today.**
2. Record a **one-minute voice memo in Thai.**
3. Do a **roleplay exercise**—order imaginary food, introduce yourself, or ask for directions.

Do this daily, and soon, **you'll be speaking Thai naturally, with confidence.**

Next up, let's push your fluency even further with full-on **Thai immersion techniques!**

CHAPTER EIGHT:
Speaking Before You're Ready

THE TINDER DATE THAT TURNED INTO A THAI POP QUIZ

I should've known something was off when she texted, "ไปกับเพื่อนนะ" before the date.

Now, my Thai wasn't **bad** at this point—but I still had gaps. And "ไปกับเพื่อนนะ" didn't raise any red flags.

I read it. I smiled. I assumed it meant **"I'm on my way."**

It did not.

It meant: **"I'm bringing my friend."**

I found this out the moment I arrived at the bar. I walked in, scanning the tables, expecting to spot **one** girl. Instead, I spotted **two.**

Both **stunning.**
Both **smirking.**
Both **staring directly at me.**

"สวัสดีค่า~" my date purred.

Her friend leaned in, tilting her head. "พูดไทยได้มั้ย?"

That's when it hit me:
This was no **regular** date—this was an **ambush.**

A **bilingual battlefield.**

And I was walking in **unarmed.**

Now, normally, I'd have **time** to think. To prepare. To carefully construct a sentence in my head before saying it out loud.

Not here.

Not with **two beautiful women staring at me, sipping their Thai milk teas, waiting for me to respond.**

I tried to play it cool.

"พูดได้นิดหน่อยครับ" (*I speak a little.*)

They both laughed.

Not the *haha, you're funny* kind of laugh.

The *oh, this is gonna be fun* kind of laugh.

Her friend, who I now realized was here **purely for entertainment,** leaned forward and fired off a question.

Fast.

Too fast.

All I caught was **"อะไร"**, which I knew meant **"what."**

I panicked.

I had **two choices:**

1. **Ask her to repeat it slower.** (Safe, logical, mature.)
2. **Laugh and nod like I understood.** (Risky, but potentially smooth.)

Guess which one I picked?

Yup.

I went **full confidence mode.**

I nodded, smiled, and let out a casual: "ใช่ครับ แน่นอน" *(Yes, of course.)*

Her eyes widened.

My date choked on her drink.

Her friend gasped and said, "จริงเหรอ?" *(Really?)*

At this point, **I knew I had made a mistake.**

A *big* mistake.

I had **no idea what I had just agreed to.**

Was it an embarrassing confession? A promise to buy all their desserts? A marriage proposal?!

My brain screamed at me to **fix it.**

So, naturally, I went for the classic **language learner survival tactic: I changed the subject.**

I took a sip of my drink, grinned, and said, "แล้วสองคนรู้จักกันได้ยังไงเหรอ?" *(So... how did you two meet?)*

They **blinked.**

They **looked at each other.**

Then, they **burst out laughing.**

Her friend clapped her hands. **"คนนี้ฉลาดดีนะ!"** *(This guy is clever!)*

Crisis **averted.**

For now.

The Lesson: Speak First, Fix Later

That night, I learned something powerful: **You don't need to be perfect to survive a conversation.**

Did I know **all the words?** No.
Did I make **tons of mistakes?** Yes.
Did I have an **amazing time anyway?** Absolutely.

Because **language isn't about perfection—it's about connection.**

And that's exactly what this chapter is about.

You don't need to wait until you **"feel ready"** to start speaking Thai.

You need to **speak first.**

Then figure out the rest as you go.

Let's dive in!

THE 'OUTPUT FIRST' APPROACH

If you're waiting until you **feel ready** to start speaking Thai fluently, I've got some bad news for you…

You'll be waiting forever.

The biggest mistake language learners make is thinking they need to study **enough grammar, enough vocabulary, enough classifiers** before they can speak. But that's **backward.**

Think about how **kids learn languages.** Nobody hands them a **500-page grammar textbook** before they start speaking. They just **blurt things out,** make tons of **mistakes,** and eventually, through trial and error, they **get it right.**

You didn't wait until you were an expert in English to start talking as a kid—so why are you doing it with Thai?

Speak First, Figure It Out Later

Let's get this straight:

You **do not** need perfect grammar to communicate.

You **do not** need a massive vocabulary to start speaking.

You **do not** need to feel "ready" before jumping in.

What you **do** need is a willingness to **sound stupid**—at least for a little while.

And guess what? That's **completely normal.**

If you can **order a coffee, ask for directions, or compliment someone's dog** (all in Thai), you've **won.** Sure, you might **butcher a few sentences,** but the other person will still **understand you.**

You'll be **speaking Thai**—and that's all that matters.

How Babies Learn Languages (And Why You Should Copy Them)

Babies don't sit around **studying tone rules or verb particles** before saying their first words.

Instead, they:

1. **Blurt out words** (often wrong).
2. **Get corrected** (but nobody expects them to be perfect).
3. **Slowly refine** what they say.

This is exactly how you should approach Thai.

Instead of **waiting to be perfect,** try saying something—**anything**—and work from there.

Would a baby say:

- *"Excuse me, father. Might I request a small portion of milk, please?"*

Nope.

They say: **"Milk!"** (Or maybe even **"Mmmilk!"** with a weird grunt).

And guess what? They **get the milk** anyway.

Your goal should be the same.

Instead of thinking:

× **"I must remember all the correct words before I speak."**

Think:

✓ **"How can I get my point across, even if my sentence isn't perfect?"**

Why Even Bad Thai Still Works

Let's say you're at a night market in Chiang Mai, and you want to say:

- **"I'm hungry."**

But you panic. You forget **how to say 'I am'** in Thai. Your brain **freezes.**

So instead, you blurt out:

× **"ฉันหิวข้าว"** (without any polite particle, and maybe with wrong tone)

Guess what? The waiter **still gets it.**

He's not going to stop and say:

- **"Ah, technically, you should say 'ผมหิวครับ' or 'หนูหิวค่ะ' depending on gender."**

No. He's going to bring you **food.**

In fact, **this is exactly how kids learn.** They say:

× "Me want cookie."

And do they get the cookie? **Yes, they do.**

The same principle applies to Thai: **Even bad Thai is still effective Thai.**

Challenge: One Full Day of Only Speaking Thai

If you want to **force your brain** to adapt to Thai faster, here's a challenge:

For one full day, you are only allowed to speak in Thai.

That means:

✓ **Narrate your day in Thai.** *(จะไปอาบน้ำ จะทำกาแฟ ต้องทำงานแล้ว)*

✓ **Talk to friends or family in Thai.** *(If they don't understand, explain it with hand gestures!)*

✓ **Order your food in Thai.** *(Even if you have to mix in pointing and miming!)*

PRO TIP: If you don't know a word, **find another way to describe it** instead of switching to English.

For example:

Instead of "bathtub," say **"that thing where I take a bath."**
Instead of "wallet," say **"that thing where I keep my money."**

By the end of the day, you'll realize something important:

- ✓ **You don't need to be perfect to speak Thai.**
- ✓ **You don't need more studying—you need more speaking.**
- ✓ **You can already communicate more than you think.**

So **stop waiting** and start speaking.

But what happens when you start speaking and suddenly freeze? Your mind goes blank, you forget the words, and panic sets in. That's completely normal—but you don't have to stay stuck.

That's where the **'2-Minute Fluency'** exercise comes in. This technique forces your brain to **keep talking,** even when you don't know the perfect words.

THE '2-MINUTE FLUENCY' EXERCISE

Picture this: You're in a conversation with a Thai speaker. You start strong. The first few words come out smoothly.

And then…

Your brain **freezes.**

You suddenly **forget a word.**

Panic sets in. You go silent, searching your memory, but nothing comes. The person stares at you, waiting. The pressure builds. Your confidence **plummets.**

THIS is what kills fluency—not lack of vocabulary, but the hesitation and silence.

The Biggest Fluency Killer: Overthinking

Most language learners assume **fluency means knowing all the words**—but that's a lie.

Fluency is about **keeping the conversation going** no matter what.

Think about native speakers. When they **forget a word,** do they panic? No. They just **describe it differently.**

For example, if an English speaker forgets the word **"thermometer"**, they might say:

✓ **"That thing you use to check if you have a fever."**

That's exactly how you should handle Thai.

So instead of freezing, train yourself to **keep talking, no matter what.**

The 2-Minute Fluency Exercise

This is the **#1 technique** to train your brain to **speak fluidly, even with limited vocabulary.**

Here's how it works:

1. **Set a timer for 2 minutes.**
2. **Pick a random topic (food, travel, your morning routine, etc.).**
3. **Start talking in Thai.**
4. **The Golden Rule: NEVER stop speaking.**

Even if you forget a word, **find another way to say it.**

Let's try it. Imagine you're talking about **what you did yesterday.**

If you forget the word "เตียง" **(bed)**, don't freeze—just **describe it:**

× **Don't say:** "Uh… um… I don't know how to say it…" *(Awkward silence…)*

✓ **Instead, say:** "ผมนอนบน... เอ่อ... สิ่งที่ใหญ่ๆ ที่คนใช้นอนตอนกลางคืน" *(I slept on... uh... the big thing people use to sleep at night.)*

It's not perfect, but **who cares?** The other person **will understand.**

Why This Exercise Works

At first, you'll **struggle.** You'll **hesitate.** You'll **feel silly.**

But if you do this **every day for a week,** something amazing will happen:

- ✓ **Your brain will stop translating.**
- ✓ **You'll get faster at describing missing words.**
- ✓ **You'll stop overthinking and just speak.**

By the end of the week, you **won't be searching for words—you'll just be talking.**

And that's the key to fluency.

Exercise: Try It Now!

Step 1: Set a 2-minute timer.
Step 2: Pick one of these topics and start speaking in Thai:

- ▹ **What you ate for breakfast.**
- ▹ **Your last vacation.**
- ▹ **Your dream job.**
- ▹ **What's in your bag right now.**
- ▹ **The last movie you watched.**

Step 3: NEVER stop speaking. If you don't know a word, **describe it another way.**

CONVERSATIONS WITH YOURSELF—THE SECRET FLUENCY HACK

What if I told you that you already have the **best Thai conversation partner?**

Someone who is **always available, never interrupts, and won't judge your mistakes?**

It's **you.**

Why Talking to Yourself in Thai Works

Most language learners believe they **can't practice speaking unless they have a partner.** That's **wrong.**

Talking to yourself in Thai **rewires your brain to think and speak naturally**—without pressure, embarrassment, or hesitation.

Think about it:

✓ **No fear of judgment** (no one is listening).
✓ **No waiting for a partner** (instant access).
✓ **No pressure to be perfect** (you can experiment freely).

By narrating your **actions, thoughts, and daily routines** in Thai, you force your brain to **use the language** instead of just passively learning it.

And guess what? It actually **works.**

How to Start Talking to Yourself in Thai

The key is **consistency.** Make it a habit—just like brushing your teeth or scrolling through your phone.

Here's how to **train your brain for fluency:**

1. Narrate Your Day in Thai

What it is: Describe what you're doing **out loud** in Thai as you go about your day.

- **When you wake up:** "จะตื่นแล้ว ง่วงจังเลย" *(I'm going to get up. I'm so sleepy.)*
- **Making coffee:** "จะชงกาแฟ ชอบกาแฟเข้มๆ มาก" *(I'm going to make coffee. I love strong coffee.)*
- **Getting dressed:** "วันนี้จะใส่อะไรดีนะ? อากาศเย็น ต้องใส่เสื้อแจ็กเก็ต" *(What should I wear today? It's cold, so I need a jacket.)*

Challenge: For one week, pick a **daily activity** (waking up, cooking, driving, working out) and **narrate it fully in Thai.**

2. The Voice Memo Method

What it is: Record yourself speaking Thai for **one minute per day**—then listen back.

Why? Because **hearing yourself** helps you:

- ✓ **Notice pronunciation mistakes.**
- ✓ **Spot common errors.**
- ✓ **Measure your progress over time.**

- ▹ **Day 1:** Introduce yourself.
- ▹ **Day 2:** Talk about your favorite food.
- ▹ **Day 3:** Describe your daily routine.
- ▹ **Day 4:** Talk about a place you'd love to visit.
- ▹ **Day 5:** Tell a short story from your life.

Challenge: Record yourself **every day for one week,** then compare Day 1 vs. Day 7. You'll be shocked at how much more natural you sound.

3. Roleplay Real Conversations

What it is: Pretend you're in real-life Thai situations and respond **out loud.**

Imagine you're:

- **Ordering coffee:** "สวัสดีครับ ขอเอากาแฟเย็นหนึ่งแก้วครับ"
- **At a hotel check-in:** "ผมมีจองไว้ในชื่อ..."
- **Asking for directions:** "ขอโทษครับ ไปสถานีรถไฟต้องไปทางไหนครับ?"
- **Making small talk:** "คุณมาจากไหน? ชอบทำอะไรเวลาว่าง?"

At first, it might feel **silly,** but **this trick will prepare you for real conversations** so when the time comes, you **won't freeze.**

Challenge: Every day, pick a **scenario** and act it out in Thai for 2 minutes.

The Moment It All Pays Off

Here's a true story from a Thai learner:

He spent **weeks** practicing how to introduce himself **alone in his room.**

One day, a Thai speaker randomly asked, **"คุณชื่ออะไร?"**

And without thinking, he **answered perfectly.**

Flawless pronunciation. Perfect grammar. No hesitation.

He even shocked **himself.**

That's the power of **talking to yourself.**

Final Thoughts

Fluency isn't about **knowing more words**—it's about **being able to use the ones you already know without hesitation.**

Talking to yourself **daily** will:

- ✓ **Boost your confidence.**
- ✓ **Make speaking feel natural.**
- ✓ **Train your brain to think in Thai.**

Challenge: For the next **7 days,** commit to **narrating your life in Thai, recording voice memos, and roleplaying daily situations.**

By the end of the week, **Thai won't feel like a foreign language anymore—it will feel like a part of you.**

But there's still one missing piece…
Can you stay fluent when the pressure's on?
That's exactly what we'll train next. Let's go!

CHAPTER NINE:
The Speed Fluency Method

THE TIME I GOT MISTAKEN FOR A FUGITIVE IN BANGKOK

It all started with a sandwich.

Not just any sandwich. A grilled pork toast from a sizzling street vendor in Victory Monument—juicy, smoky, and slathered in chili sauce, all wrapped in a crispy slice of bread.

I had just finished filming a video downtown and was starving. As I took the first glorious bite, I noticed a guy nearby staring at me. Not just a quick glance—*staring*, like he recognized me from somewhere. I wiped my mouth. Had he seen my YouTube?

He stepped closer. "เฮ้... ใช่คุณหรือเปล่า?"

I blinked. Was that slang? "เอ่อ... อะไรนะครับ?"

"ใช่เลย! นายคือคนนั้นจากคลิปนั่น!" he shouted, pointing at me with a grin like he'd just solved a murder mystery.

People turned to look. Phones came out. I smiled awkwardly, still chewing, when another guy joined him.
"เฮ้เพื่อน! เราเห็นนายใน TikTok! นายอยู่ทุกที่เลย!"

Okay. Cool. I was famous in Thailand now. I gave a thumbs-up and kept chewing.

Then it turned.

A third guy ran up, phone in hand. He shoved it in my face. "นี่นายใช่มั้ยที่ขโมยมือถือผู้หญิงคนนี้!?" On screen was a blurry photo of someone who *kind of* looked like me… running.

Wait. What?

“ไม่ๆๆ” I stammered, mouth full of grilled pork. “ผมไม่ได้ขโมยอะไรเลย ผมเป็น... ยูทูบเบอร์ครับ”

“โกหก!” he snapped. “ก็ดูหมวกดิ เหมือนกันเป๊ะ”

I looked down. Damn it. I was wearing a black cap—just like the guy in the blurry video.

Suddenly, I had a small crowd. People speaking rapid-fire Thai, way faster than my brain could keep up. I caught fragments:

“—หน้าคล้ายเลยอะ—”

“—เรียกตำรวจมา—”

“—ไวรัลเต็มโซเชียล—”

I tried to explain, but my Thai was disintegrating. Words jammed in my mouth. I couldn’t find the right tenses. I wanted to say “I think you have the wrong person,” but it came out something like: “เอ่อ... ผม... คิดว่า... ไม่ใช่ผมครับ” Which sounded exactly like something a guilty tourist would say.

Finally, I did the only thing I could.

I started talking as fast as I could in the most over-the-top, farang-accented Thai possible: “สวัสดีครับ ผมชื่อเอเดรียน เป็นยูทูบเบอร์ ไม่ใช่ขโมย ผมแค่มากินขนมปังหมู ผมรักเมืองไทยมาก ผมสาบานเลยว่าผมไม่ได้ขโมยอะไร อย่าเรียกตำรวจเลยครับ ผมกลัว แล้วก็มือผมเปื้อนซอสด้วย”

Silence.

Someone giggled. Another guy cracked a smile.

"เขาแค่บื้อเฉยๆ," someone muttered. (He's just a dumbass.)

And just like that, they backed off.

I took a deep breath. The sandwich was cold. But I had never felt more alive.

And that, my friend, was the day I learned: in real life, there's no time for perfect grammar. You've just gotta *go*. No hesitation. No filters. **Just speak.**

FAST VS. SLOW THINKING – TRAINING YOUR BRAIN FOR FLOW

When people hear "fluency," they often imagine someone rattling off perfect sentences at lightning speed. But true fluency isn't about talking fast—it's about **thinking fast.** It's about keeping the flow going even when you don't know the exact word, phrase, or verb tense. It's about confidence, not perfection.

And the key to this is **shifting from "slow thinking" to "fast thinking."**

What Does "Slow Thinking" Look Like?

Picture this: you're in the middle of a conversation and someone asks, "เมื่อสุดสัปดาห์ที่แล้วคุณทำอะไรบ้าง?" (What did you do last weekend?)

You panic. Your brain starts processing like this:

Okay, that's past tense… Wait, should I use แล้ว (already) or เคย (used to)? Is it ทำ or ไปทำ...? What if I say it wrong?

By the time you decide on a sentence, the conversation has already moved on.

This is slow thinking. It's what happens when your brain is stuck in analysis mode instead of response mode.

What Is "Fast Thinking" in Thai?

Fast thinking is when you **bypass the analysis** and just **respond with what you know**—even if it's not perfect.

A native might ask:

- "คุณชอบดูหนังไหม?" (Do you like movies?)

Fast-thinking response:

- "ชอบมากเลยครับ ผมไปดูหนังวันเสาร์ที่ผ่านมา หนังแปลกดีแต่ก็สนุกนะครับ"
  (Yes, I really like it. I went to see a movie last Saturday. It was weird, but enjoyable.)

Maybe your grammar wasn't flawless. Maybe you hesitated on "สนุก." But the point is—you **kept the conversation going.**

The Real Goal: Conversational Flow

Fluency isn't about never making mistakes. It's about creating momentum.

Native-level fluency = responding instinctively.
It's reacting the same way you do when someone tosses you a ball—you don't pause and calculate physics. You **just catch it.**

The goal is to build those **reflexes** in Thai.

Common Slow-Thinking Traps

Here are a few habits that kill your fluency flow:

- **Over-conjugating mid-sentence:**
  "I... uh... will have gone... no wait... I will be going..."

- **Translation tunnel vision:**
  Thinking in English → Translating to Thai → Rearranging the sentence

- **Second-guessing everything:**
  "Should I use classifier 'เล่ม' *or* 'อัน'*? Is it polite enough? Should I say* ค่ะ *or* ครับ*?"*

These traps slow you down and **create more self-doubt than clarity.**

Break the Hesitation: Fast-Flow Mindset Drills

Let's train your brain to think quickly and speak fluidly. Try these:

1. **Improv Word Toss**
   Choose a random Thai noun (e.g., "หนังสือ"). Now say 5 things about it as fast as possible:
   "ผมชอบหนังสือเล่มนี้. มันน่าสนใจ. เกี่ยวกับการท่องเที่ยว. ผมอ่านอยู่ตอนนี้. ผมซื้อเมื่อวาน."

2. **Warm-Up Games**
   Before speaking practice, say 10 basic Thai phrases *without pausing*. Don't aim for perfection—aim for speed.

3. **Describe What You See**
   Wherever you are, name and describe things around you—เร็วๆ. "โต๊ะ. สีขาว. มีเอกสาร. มีแก้วน้ำ. แก้วน้ำสีฟ้า."

Challenge: 5-Minute "No Pause" Self-Conversation

Set a timer for 5 minutes. Talk to yourself in Thai without stopping. It can be about your day, your breakfast, your plans—**anything.**

Rules:

- **No English allowed.**
- If you forget a word, **describe it or work around it.**
- Don't pause. Don't overthink.

Example:

- "วันนี้ผมตื่นสายหน่อย เพราะ... เอ่อ.., เมื่อคืนนอนไม่ค่อยดี เตียงมัน... อะไรดี... ร้อนมากเลย แล้วก็ไปที่ครัว ทำกาแฟ..."

By the end, you'll feel the gears turning faster—and that's the point.

FLASH CONVERSATIONS – SIMULATE REAL-LIFE THAI UNDER PRESSURE

Learning Thai in a classroom or from an app is one thing. But real Thai—the kind you hear in a Bangkok street market, in a tuk-tuk, or while ordering food at a night bazaar in Chiang Mai—is a whole different beast.

It's fast.
It's messy.
It's unpredictable.

And if you're not ready for it, you'll freeze.

That's why you need **Flash Conversations**—rapid, high-pressure drills that mimic the chaos of real life. Think of it like training for a **verbal boxing match.** You don't know what punch is coming next… you just have to react.

Why Speed and Pressure Matter

In real conversations, no one gives you time to pause and think. You don't get to quietly review grammar charts in your head. You either **respond quickly,** or the moment passes.

Flash Conversations train your brain to think on its feet.

You learn to:

- Process questions instantly
- Answer even if you don't know every word
- Stay calm when your brain wants to panic

And the best part? You can train this skill **without** a conversation partner.

How to Simulate Flash Conversations at Home

Here's how to bring the pressure of the real world into your practice routine:

1. **Use Flashcards or Apps**
   Write 20 random Thai questions on cards (or generate them with an app). Flip one over. You have 5 seconds to answer.

2. **Use ChatGPT or AI Tools**
   Prompt: "Give me 10 random Thai questions for rapid-fire conversation." Boom—you're in business.

3. **Set a Timer**
   Limit yourself to 60 seconds. Try to answer as many questions as you can. No pausing, no translating—just go.

Sample Flash Conversation: At a Café

You're at a café in Thailand. The waiter is rapid-fire. Your job? Keep up.

Waiter: รับอะไรดีครับ? (What would you like?)
You: เอากาแฟเย็นแก้วนึงครับ (I'll have an iced coffee, please.)

Waiter: หวานมาก หวานน้อย หรือไม่หวาน? (Very sweet, less sweet, or no sugar?)
You:: หวานน้อยครับ (Less sweet, please.)

Waiter: ทานที่นี่หรือเอากลับครับ? (Dine-in or take away?)
You: เอากลับครับ (Take away, please.)

Waiter: รับอะไรเพิ่มอีกไหมครับ? (Would you like anything else?)
You: ไม่ครับ แค่นี้พอ (No, that's all.)

Now do it again—faster.

Drill: The "Rapid 10"

Goal: Answer 10 questions in 60 seconds.

You can use:

- A friend to read questions out loud
- An AI chatbot to send questions one by one
- A random question generator app

Sample questions:

1. คุณอยู่ที่ไหน?
2. วันนี้กินอะไรไปบ้าง?
3. คุณมีพี่น้องไหม?
4. วันหยุดชอบทำอะไร?
5. คุณชอบดูหนังไหม?
6. ฟังเพลงแนวไหนบ้าง?
7. ตอนนี้เรียนหรือทำงานอยู่?
8. เคยไปต่างประเทศไหม?
9. อาหารจานโปรดของคุณคืออะไร?
10. พรุ่งนี้จะทำอะไร?

Even if you mess up—**keep going.** The goal isn't perfection. It's survival.

Why This Works (and Why It's Fun)

You will:

- Forget words
- Mix up tones
- Say weird things like "ฉันร้อน" when you meant "ฉันหนาว" (I'm hot instead of I'm cold)

And it's okay. That's the point.

Flash Conversations are messy on purpose. They train you for the real world—where native speakers won't wait for you to find the perfect classifier or verb aspect.

Final Challenge: Daily Flash Conversation

For the next 7 days:

- Pick a topic (travel, food, daily life, hobbies)
- Set a timer for 2 minutes
- Ask yourself (or have an app ask you) questions on that topic
- Answer them as fast as you can—no pausing

Do this and soon, Thai won't feel like a slow puzzle you're solving. It'll feel like a language you *live in.*

REACT, DON'T TRANSLATE – HOW TO BUILD REFLEXES IN THAI

Let's face it—your brain loves being in control.

It loves pausing to think, analyze, and make everything perfect.

But when it comes to Thai fluency? That perfection-seeking brain is slowing you down.

The key to real fluency isn't just knowing more Thai—it's knowing how to **react in Thai.** Instantly. Naturally. Without English getting in the way.

English = The Middleman

Every time you hear Thai, your brain has two choices:

1. **Translate into English,** think of an answer, then translate it back.
2. **React directly in Thai,** the way native speakers do.

Option one? It's like ordering food from a waiter who calls another waiter who then walks into the kitchen. Slow. Confusing. Frustrating.

Option two? It's like making your own coffee. Fast. Direct. Efficient.

If you want to speak fluidly, you have to **cut out the middleman.**

Fluency = Reflexes, Not Logic

Think of it like catching a ball.

When someone throws it at you, you don't pause and think:
"Okay, this is a spherical object moving at me with velocity... I should extend my hand at a 45-degree angle..."

You just **catch it.** Instinctively.

That's how Thai should feel.

So how do we build those reflexes?

Let's train.

Rapid Reflex Training Drills

Here are three fun ways to stop translating and start reacting:

1. The Yes/No Snap Game

Goal: Train instant responses to simple questions.

How: Ask yourself (or have someone ask you) rapid-fire yes/no questions in Thai. You must answer in less than **1 second.**

Examples:

- คุณชอบกาแฟไหม?
- คุณง่วงไหม?
- คุณอยู่กรุงเทพใช่ไหม?
- คุณมีพี่น้องไหม?

Your brain shouldn't translate these—it should just spit out:

- ใช่
- ไม่ใช่
- นิดหน่อย
- แน่นอน

Do this daily and you'll rewire your brain for **snap reactions.**

2. Either/Or Lightning Rounds

Goal: Build speed and confidence with preferences.

How: Ask either/or questions and answer without hesitation.

Examples:

- ชาเย็นหรือกาแฟเย็น?
- ทะเลหรือภูเขา?
- กรุงเทพหรือเชียงใหม่?
- หมาหรือแมว?

Say the first thing that comes to mind in Thai.

Even if it's "ทั้งคู่" (both), say something. Just **don't freeze.**

3. Pause & React (Video Edition)

Goal: Simulate real conversation pace.

How: Watch a Thai YouTube video, lakorn (Thai drama), or podcast. Pause after every sentence and **respond** to it out loud.

It doesn't matter if your answer is simple. The goal is to **think in Thai** and keep the pace moving.

Example:

- **Speaker:** "เมื่อวานคุณทำอะไร?" (What did you do yesterday?)
- You: "ไปฟิตเนส" (I went to the gym.)
- **Speaker:** "แล้วหลังจากนั้นล่ะ?" (And after that?)
- You: "ไปกินข้าวกับเพื่อน" (I had dinner with friends.)

Think of it like boxing drills—but for your mouth and brain.

Real-Life Reflex Saves

Here's where reflexes really matter.

Imagine:

- You're in a BTS station in Bangkok. The train's arriving in 2 minutes. The staff is giving you directions in Thai. You need to react.

- You're on a date at a night market. She smiles and says, "คุณชอบขนมไทยแบบไหนมากที่สุด?" (What kind of Thai dessert do you like most?)

- You're checking into a guesthouse in Krabi, and the receptionist starts rattling off info about breakfast, Wi-Fi, and scooter rental.

If you **pause to translate,** you'll miss half the conversation.

If you **react,** you stay in the flow—and that's fluency.

Final Exercise: The "1-Second Reflex" Challenge

Let's do it right now.

Rules:

- No thinking.
- No translating.
- Just answer.

Answer each of these Thai questions in 1 second or less:

1. คุณชื่ออะไร? → ________
2. มาจากไหน? → ________
3. หิวไหม? → ________
4. ตอนนี้กี่โมง? → ________
5. ชอบทำอะไร? → ________
6. อยู่ที่ไหน? → ________
7. ง่วงไหม? → ________
8. วันนี้วันอะไร? → ________
9. ชอบฟังเพลงไหม? → ________
10. ชอบชาเย็นหรือกาแฟเย็น? → ________
11. ทำอาหารเป็นไหม? → ________
12. กำลังเรียนภาษาไทยอยู่ใช่ไหม? → ________
13. เมื่อวานทำอะไร? → ________
14. ทำงานที่ไหน? → ________
15. อาหารจานโปรดของคุณคืออะไร? → ________
16. มีสัตว์เลี้ยงไหม? → ________
17. พร้อมหรือยัง? → ________
18. เสาร์-อาทิตย์ทำอะไร? → ________
19. สีโปรดของคุณคือสีอะไร? → ________
20. ตื่นกี่โมง? → ________

If you hesitated on more than 3… great! You've found your next fluency workout.

Final Takeaway

Fluency isn't a test. It's a **reflex.**

You don't pass it—you train it. Not by being perfect, but by responding without hesitation.

But real fluency isn't just about what you say out loud…

It's about how you think when no one's listening.

That's where we're headed next.

CHAPTER TEN:
Training Your Inner Voice in Thai

THE TIME I GOT CAUGHT IN A LIE... WITH MYSELF

I was in Chiang Mai, sitting at a quiet café near the old city moat, enjoying a slow lunch. The kind where you don't look at the time because the breeze is soft, the khao soi is spicy, and there's nowhere else you need to be.

That's when it happened.

A woman with fire-red lipstick and oversized sunglasses sat down across from me.

Uninvited.

"I know you," she said in Thai.

I blinked. "Sorry?"

She didn't budge. "From the bar last night. You said your name was David."

That's when I panicked.

Because I hadn't been to a bar. I hadn't told anyone my name was David. And definitely not in Thai.

But for some reason—**my brain instantly flipped to Thai mode.**

"ไม่ครับ ผมชื่อเอเดรียน" I replied, trying to laugh it off.

She narrowed her eyes. "Oh, *now* you speak Thai."

It was like my brain was having two different conversations at once—one in English frantically asking *What the hell is going on?*—and the other in Thai saying *keep your cool, stay in the flow, don't mess this up.*

I realized I was having a full-blown internal argument.

In two languages.

Outwardly, I was calm. Inside, I was a bilingual battlefield.

And in that moment, something clicked: **the real test of fluency isn't speaking—it's thinking in Thai, especially under pressure.**

Your inner voice, that silent narrator in your head? That's your fluency engine.

And this chapter is all about training that voice until it *thinks, argues,* and *narrates* entirely in Thai—no English middleman.

Let's go!

THE SILENT THINKING EXERCISE

Let's level up.

By now, you've spoken to yourself in Thai. You've narrated your day. You've recorded voice memos, played fluency games, and maybe even argued with your reflection in the mirror.

But there's one skill that separates good learners from unstoppable ones:

Thinking in Thai—even when it's completely silent.

No mouth. No voice. No notebook.
Just you.
And your inner voice.

Why Silent Thinking Is a Fluency Superpower

Here's the truth: **fluency doesn't happen when you speak—it happens before.**

It happens in the split-second before the words come out of your mouth. And that moment—when your brain chooses what to say—is exactly what this exercise trains.

Most learners skip this step. They focus on what they *say out loud,* but never train the quiet voice inside their head. That voice—the one narrating your life when you're walking, cooking, scrolling, or staring out a bus window—is where **true fluency begins.**

Silent thinking bypasses your vocal cords and your writing hand. It forces your **brain** to get fluent.

No excuses. No performance anxiety. Just mental reps.

How It Works

Set aside just **15 minutes a day** for one simple rule:

Think only in Thai.
No English. No translating. No "What's that word again?" Just keep going.

You don't need to say anything aloud. You don't even need to move your lips.

Just sit—or walk—and narrate your thoughts in your head, in real time.

Start with simple thoughts:

- "ฉันจะไปทำกาแฟ"
- "หลังจากนั้น ฉันต้องตอบข้อความนั้น"
- "สงสัยว่าฝนจะตกตอนเย็นไหม"

Over time, you'll naturally graduate to more complex reflections:

- "ทำไมฉันถึงยังผลัดงานนั้นอยู่?"
- "บางทีฉันควรพูดอีกแบบในบทสนทนานั้น"
- "วันนี้รู้สึกมีแรงจูงใจมากกว่าเมื่อวาน อาจเป็นเพราะนอนดีขึ้นก็ได้"

Thought Starters to Get You Going

If your mind goes blank, use these as prompts:

- **Plan your day**
  "วันนี้ฉันจะตื่นเช้า ไปฟิตเนส แล้วกลับมาทำงานต่อ"

- **Reflect on a memory**
  "ฉันนึกถึงตอนที่ไปเที่ยวเชียงใหม่ อากาศดี ผู้คนน่ารัก ทุกอย่างรู้สึกอบอุ่น"

- **Mentally walk through a process**
  "เริ่มจากต้มน้ำ ใส่บะหมี่ รอประมาณห้านาที..."

- **Silent workout or meditation narration**
  "หายใจเข้าลึก ๆ รู้สึกถึงร่างกายของฉัน มีความตึงที่ไหล่ขวา..."

- **Inner monologue while commuting**
  "รถบนถนนเยอะมาก คนน่าจะรีบไปทำงาน ฉันควรเดินเลี่ยงไปอีกทางดีกว่า"

Advanced Bonus: Meditation Mode

This is where things get real.

Try meditating, stretching, or working out—**while keeping your internal thoughts in Thai.**

Example:

- “หายใจเข้า... หายใจออก...”
- “รู้สึกถึงขาและน้ำหนักตัวที่ลงพื้น”
- “อยู่กับปัจจุบัน ไม่มีอะไรสำคัญไปกว่านี้”

Doing this conditions your brain to **default to Thai,** even when you're relaxed, distracted, or deeply focused. That's fluency on autopilot.

Silent Thinking Challenge

Here's your 3-part mission:

1. **Set a 15-minute timer** every day.
   During that time, your brain is Thai-only territory.

2. **Track your slips.**
   When your brain switches to English, **notice it—then gently switch back.** No self-judgment.

3. **Write down tricky thoughts.**
   If you couldn't say something in Thai, make a note. Look it up later and try again the next day.

Silent thinking isn't just a cool exercise—it's a **fluency multiplier.**

It builds real-time recall. It rewires your brain.
And it makes Thai part of your *actual* inner world.

Now that you can think silently in Thai… what happens when you start **arguing** with yourself in Thai?

Let's find out in the next section.

ARGUING WITH YOURSELF IN THAI

It's time to stop being polite… to yourself.

No more safe phrases. No more simple thoughts.

This section is about one thing:

Debate. Drama. Fluent inner chaos.

Because if you can **argue with yourself in Thai,** you can survive *anything.*

Why Internal Debates Supercharge Fluency

Most language learners get good at small talk.

"Where are you from?"
"I like your shirt."
"What do you do?"

But real fluency isn't built on polite sentences. It's built on **opinions**—and the ability to express them quickly, clearly, and with conviction.

Arguing with yourself in Thai helps you:

- Use advanced, emotionally charged language.
- Practice connecting ideas with logic and fluency.
- Shift perspectives mid-conversation—without breaking flow.
- Push your brain out of "tourist mode" and into "real speaker mode."

Think of it as a mental gym session—but in Thai.

How It Works

Pick a topic. Any topic.
Then—take both sides.

You're no longer just one person—you're **both debaters.**

Go back and forth, in your mind (or aloud if you're feeling spicy), switching between opposing views. Defend. Attack. Rant. Backpedal. Just keep going—in Thai.

Fun & Silly Debate Topics to Start With

You don't need to start with philosophy or politics. Start with something dumb. In fact, **the sillier, the better.**

Try these:

- ▹ **Should pineapple go on pizza?**
  "แน่นอนสิ มันหวาน มันเค็ม มันลงตัวสุด ๆ"
  "ลงตัว!? นี่มันอาชญากรรมทางอาหาร!"

- **Is living in Chiang Mai better than Bangkok?**
  “เชียงใหม่สงบ มีธรรมชาติ อากาศดี...”
  “แต่กรุงเทพฯ มีชีวิตชีวา เดินทางสะดวก ร้านอาหารเยอะ!”

- **Should you date a local to learn Thai faster?**
  “แน่นอน เป็นวิธีที่ดีที่สุดในการเรียนรู้”
  “แล้วถ้าเขาทำให้เธอเสียใจล่ะ?”
  “ก็ดี จะได้เรียนรู้คำศัพท์เกี่ยวกับความรู้สึกด้วย!”

- **Is your accent charming or cringe?**
  “สำเนียงฉันน่ารักมาก! คนชอบนะ”
  “ไม่นะ ฟังดูเหมือนฝรั่งหลงทาง ฝึกเพิ่มด่วน!”

Seriously, you’ll be surprised how often these debates spiral into hilarious tangents—and how much Thai you pull out of your brain when you stop holding back.

Optional Mode: Debate in the Mirror

Want to raise the stakes?

Stand in front of a mirror.

Point at yourself. Make faces. Gesture wildly like you’re in a Thai lakorn. Talk with your hands like an auntie arguing at a street market.

Pretend it’s real.
Because when your brain *believes* it’s a real conversation, it works harder—and gets sharper.

Reflect, Review, Repeat

Want to level up the impact of this exercise?

1. **Write down your best arguments.**
   Focus on how you expressed your points and what phrases came naturally.

2. **Notice gaps.**
   Couldn't find a word for "benefits"? Didn't know how to say "that doesn't make sense"?

3. **Look them up, learn them, and come back for round 2.**

Every time you debate, you'll speak faster, think deeper, and use more colorful Thai.

Your Challenge

- Pick **1 new debate topic** each day for the next 5 days.
- Spend 10 minutes arguing both sides—in your head, out loud, or in front of a mirror.
- Write down or record a few of your best arguments.
- Reflect on which vocab you're missing. Go learn it.

Final Takeaway

This isn't just about fluency. It's about **mental agility.**
It's about being able to **fight with yourself in Thai**… and win.

Up next, we'll explore how **emotions and fluency** go hand in hand—and why tapping into how you *feel* could be the fluency breakthrough you've been waiting for.

Let's go!

CHAPTER ELEVEN:
Emotion and Fluency

THE TIME I CRIED IN THAI

It started with a girl. Doesn't it always?

Her name was Mali. Thai. Artist. Eyes that looked like they could read your entire browser history. We met at an outdoor art festival in Chiang Mai—she caught me staring at a mural of a golden elephant riding a motorcycle through space. She smiled. I panicked. And out came the most awkward sentence I've ever said:

"ตาของคุณเหมือน... สัญญาณไวไฟ"
(Your eyes are like… WiFi.)

She blinked.

Then laughed.

Somehow, that was enough to get me invited to her open-mic poetry night. In Thai.

Now, here's the thing—I had been learning Thai for months. But poetry? Emotional nuance? Metaphors that made sense? I was more prepared to order pad krapow than decode the soul of Sunthorn Phu.

Still, I showed up. Candlelit courtyard. Paper lanterns swaying above. A man playing the khim on a wooden stool.

And then Mali took the mic.

She read a poem about heartbreak, forgiveness, and the feeling of walking home alone in the rain when Chiang Mai smells like wet frangipani and something unspoken. At least, that's what I think it was about. I only understood half the words—but all of the feelings.

My throat tightened. Goosebumps. And then, to my horror... my eyes welled up.

I wasn't sad. I wasn't even sure what she said. But her rhythm, her voice, the raw energy—it hit me. Not in the mind. In the gut.

That night, I realized something no textbook had ever taught me:

You don't need to understand every word to feel something. And once you feel it—you'll remember it forever.

Let's talk about that.
In this chapter, we're diving into why **emotion is the secret ingredient** to unforgettable Thai.

Let's go!

WHY EMOTION SUPERCHARGES YOUR MEMORY

Ever notice how you still remember the lyrics to a breakup song from 10 years ago—but can't recall what you ate for lunch two days ago?

That's not a memory problem. That's a *feeling* problem.

Our brains aren't wired to retain boring, neutral information. They're designed to hold on to **moments that made us feel something**—especially moments tied to **emotion, embarrassment, joy,** or **survival-level panic.**

And when it comes to learning Thai? Emotion is your secret weapon.

The Brain Loves Emotionally Charged Input

In neuroscience, there's a well-studied phenomenon: **emotional arousal increases memory retention.** In simple terms, when your heart is beating faster, your brain is paying attention.

The amygdala (your brain's emotion processor) basically sends a group text to the rest of your brain saying: "Hey! This moment matters. Save it."

That's why you vividly remember your first kiss, your worst presentation, or the time you nearly got scammed in a night market in Bangkok—but not the details of that grammar worksheet you did last week.

So let's use that to your advantage.

Real-Life Thai You'll Never Forget

Want to remember new words forever? Feel something while you're learning them.

Here are some *unforgettable* emotional-Thai moments learners have shared:

- A guy tried to compliment a woman's dress in Chiang Rai but instead said, **"คุณดูเหมือนจะท้อง"** *("You look pregnant")*... when he meant "shy." The shame is burned into his brain—and so is the word **ท้อง**.

- A woman had her first kiss in Phuket under the stars and remembered every word he said, especially **"คุณสวยมาก"** *("You're very beautiful")*. She says it's the reason she fell in love with Thai—and him.

- A traveler missed the last minivan out of Pai, got stranded, and had to ask for help in broken Thai. She never forgot **"ฉันหลงทาง"** *("I'm lost")* after that.

These moments weren't studied in a textbook. They were **felt.** And that's why they stuck.

Use Your Feelings—Write in Thai When It Counts

You don't have to wait for a dramatic scene to make Thai emotional.

You can *create* emotional memory by journaling in Thai during moments that already matter to you.

- Heart pounding before a big event? Write about it in Thai.
- Just had a magical date or a terrible day at work? Capture it in Thai.
- Feeling excited, nervous, heartbroken, confused? Perfect. That's fuel.

Bonus tip: Even if you don't know all the words, write how it *felt.* Your brain will do the heavy lifting.

Mini Exercise: Total Emotion

Step 1: Think of a moment in your life that made you feel something powerful. It could be funny, romantic, stressful—doesn't matter.
Step 2: Write a short paragraph about that moment in Thai. Use simple words. No perfection required.
Step 3: Read it back to yourself—*feel* it again. Lock it in.

Example:

- "ตอนที่ฉันบอกลาเพื่อนสนิทที่สนามบิน ฉันรู้สึกเหมือนมีช่องว่างในใจ ฉันพูดไม่มาก แค่ 'ดูแลตัวเองนะ'... แต่มันเจ็บมาก"
  ("When I said goodbye to my best friend at the airport, I felt an emptiness in my chest. I didn't say much, just 'Take care'... but those words hurt.")

Now those words are yours. You *lived* them. You won't forget them.

MUSIC, COMEDY, AND DRAMA—LEARNING THROUGH FEELING

Thai isn't just a language you speak.
It's a language you **feel.**

It flirts. It cries. It yells. It laughs so hard it spills iced Thai tea on the floor.

And if you're only studying Thai with grammar drills and flashcards… you're missing the *heart* of it.

Because buried inside every lakorn meltdown, every luk thung lyric, every stand-up punchline…

...is a chance to learn Thai that sticks—because it *moved* you.

Let's dive in.

Music: The Soundtrack of Your Vocabulary

Want to remember Thai vocabulary for life?
Wrap it in **melody and heartbreak.**

There's a reason you still know the lyrics to songs you haven't heard in years.

Your brain processes music *emotionally.* It bypasses logic and drills the words straight into your long-term memory.

Examples:

- **Palmy** crooning “คิดถึงแต่เธอ... คิดถึงแทบบ้า” ("I only think of you… it’s driving me crazy.")
  Boom—instant lesson on คิดถึง = **to miss someone.**

- Or a line from a **heartbreak anthem:** “เจ็บนี้อีกนาน... ไม่ลืมง่ายๆ” (“This pain will last… I won’t forget easily.”)
  You might cry, smile, or Google the lyrics. Either way—**you’ll remember it.**

Tip: Look up the lyrics while listening. Sing along. Feel ridiculous. That’s the point.

Lakorns: Over-the-Top = Over-the-Moon Retention

Thai soap operas (lakorns) are **dramatic, ridiculous,** and **perfect** for learning.

Why? Because every scene is loaded with:

- **Repetition** (they say everything three times with dramatic pauses)
- **Emotion** (slaps, betrayals, screaming “ทำไมถึงทำกับฉันแบบนี้!?” into the thunderstorm)
- **Everyday language,** said loudly and slowly for dramatic effect

You’ll hear phrases like:

- “อย่ามาโกหกฉัน!” – Don’t lie to me!
- “ฉันสาบาน!” – I swear!
- “ฉันท้องแล้ว!” – I’m pregnant!

Watch a few episodes, and soon you'll be saying "ทำไมถึงทำกับฉันแบบนี้ ภูผา!?" ("How could you do this to me, Phupha!?") without even thinking.

Pro Tip: Watch with Thai subtitles—*not* English. You're not there to translate. You're there to feel the fire.

Comedy: Culture, Wordplay, and Belly Laughs

Thai stand-up comedy teaches you more than just slang.

It trains your ear to:

- Recognize **tone**
- Understand **timing**
- Catch **double meanings**
- Notice **regional expressions** that *don't* show up in textbooks

Comedians like:

- **Udom Taephanich** – witty, relatable, master of facial expression
- **Note Udom** – fast-paced jokes, plays with words and tones
- **The Pangpond Show** – a mix of sketch and stand-up humor with punchy slang

You may not catch every joke at first—but when you do, *you'll remember it forever.*

Bonus Benefit: Comedy helps you laugh at your own mistakes—which is essential when you're learning a new language.

Mini Exercise: Feel It, Then Speak It

1. Pick a Thai song, scene, or comedy bit that **made you feel something.**
2. Rewatch or relisten with Thai subtitles.
3. Then answer these two prompts—in Thai or "Thanglish":

- เกิดอะไรขึ้น? (What happened?)
- ทำไมถึงรู้สึกแบบนั้น? (Why did it make you feel something?)

Example:

- ฉันดูฉากในเรื่อง "บุพเพสันนิวาส" ที่พระเอกจากไป มันเศร้ามาก น้ำตาซึมเลย แล้วก็ได้เรียนรู้คำว่า "จากกันด้วยดี" (Parted on good terms).

By putting words to what you feel—you make them *yours.*

Music, drama, comedy—these aren't "extras."
They're emotional **shortcuts to fluency.**

And when you start feeling Thai instead of just learning it?
That's when things really start to click.

MAKE THAI PERSONAL

Here's a secret most Thai learners miss:

It's not just about how *much* you know.
It's about how *much it means to you.*

You could memorize a thousand Thai words about banking, legal jargon, or agricultural exports...

But if none of it matters to your life, your brain's going to forget it faster than you can say "น่าเบื่อจัง" (I'm bored).

Want words to stick?

Tie them to **your story.**
Your goals. Your heartbreaks. Your sense of humor. Your "why."

Personalize Your Vocabulary

You don't need to learn every Thai word under the sun.

But you *should* learn the words that light you up.

- Are you a traveler? Learn words like กระเป๋าเดินทาง, เกสต์เฮาส์, แผนที่, ผจญภัย, เที่ยวแบบแบกเป้.
- Are you a romantic? Learn คิดถึง, อยากเจอ, กอด, ออกเดท, จูบแอบๆ.

- Obsessed with business? Learn ธุรกิจ, เริ่มต้นกิจการ, การขาย, ลูกค้า, เป้าหมาย.

Language becomes powerful when it helps you *express yourself,* not just pass a test.

Link Words to Personal Experiences

The moment you connect a word to your own **emotion, memory, or dream,** it becomes unforgettable.

Let's say you learned the word บรรลุ (to achieve).
Don't just memorize it. Tie it to something real.

Example:

- "ฉันอยากบรรลุความฝันที่จะย้ายไปอยู่ที่เชียงใหม่"
  (I want to achieve my dream of moving to Chiang Mai.)

Now บรรลุ isn't just a verb. It's *your* verb.

Tip: The weirder or more emotional the memory, the more it sticks. Think: first love, awkward date, amazing vacation, terrible hostel roommate, your grandma's cooking.

Affirmations in Thai = Emotional Fluency

You already talk to yourself.
Why not do it in Thai?

Saying positive, powerful things in Thai builds more than language—it builds **identity.**

Start your mornings by looking in the mirror and saying:

- ฉันทำได้ (I can do it.)
- ฉันกำลังเปลี่ยนชีวิตของตัวเอง (I'm changing my life.)
- ฉันกำลังพัฒนาตัวเองทุกวัน (I'm getting better every day.)
- ฉันกำลังเรียนภาษาไทยแบบแชมป์เปี้ยน (I'm learning Thai like a champion.)
- ไม่มีอะไรหยุดฉันได้ (Nothing can stop me.)

It might feel silly at first.
But over time, you're not just learning Thai—you're becoming someone who *thinks and believes in Thai.*

Exercise: Make It Real, Make It Yours

1. Think of a personal goal, dream, or life change you're working toward.
2. Translate it into Thai—however messy or imperfect.
3. Say it out loud, write it on a sticky note, or record it as a voice memo.

Example:

- “ฉันเรียนภาษาไทยเพราะอยากมีชีวิตที่สุดยอดในกรุงเทพฯ”
(I'm learning Thai because I want to have an incredible life in Bangkok.)

Repeat it every morning for a week.

Bonus: Pair it with music, a Thai quote, or a picture that inspires you. The more senses and emotions you involve, the deeper the connection.

Final Thoughts

When Thai becomes personal, it stops being “just a language.”
It becomes a **mirror,** a **bridge,** a **tool** to build your dream life.

And the more you use it to talk about *you*—your goals, your beliefs, your mess-ups, your victories—the faster you'll grow.

But there's one final level left to master…

Not just thinking in Thai—but *playing* with it.
Understanding jokes, sarcasm, double meanings, and regional quirks like a native.

Let's take that final leap!

CHAPTER TWELVE:

Beyond Fluency – Thinking Like a Native

THE TIME I GOT ROASTED BY A GROUP OF THAIS — AND DIDN'T REALIZE IT

Bangkok. Midnight.

I was at a tiny local bar tucked behind a soi in the Ari neighborhood. You know the type — low lights, sticky floor, faded Singha beer posters peeling off the walls, and a jukebox playing only 90s Thai rock ballads. I had come to meet up with some new friends I'd made at a Thai-English language exchange earlier that week.

There were five of them — all native Thais. Loud, fast-talking, full of inside jokes. I was the only foreigner. And the only one not laughing.

At first, everything was going fine. I was nodding along, catching enough words to feel like I was keeping up. I even dropped a few confident "ใช่เลย!" and "จริงเหรอ?" to sound local.

But then something happened.

One of the guys, Peerapong, raised his beer and said:

"ไอ้นี่ปากหวานยิ่งกว่าน้ำตาลปี๊บ!"

Everyone burst into laughter.

I smiled politely. No idea what he meant. Sweeter than what?

Then Fon leaned in and added, "ใช่ๆ แล้วก็มือไวเหมือนแมว!"

Quick hands like a cat? Wait—is that… a compliment?

Everyone laughed harder.

I tried to laugh too, but inside I felt like I had just stepped into a linguistic escape room with zero clues.

Then came the final blow. Peerapong pointed at me again and said:

"ไอ้ฝรั่งนี่แม่งน่ารักว่ะ!"

Another round of laughter.

Now I *knew* I was the punchline — but I still had no idea why.

I took a sip of my beer, looked around the room, and asked the only logical question:

"...น้ำตาลปี๊บคืออะไรอะ?"

Silence.

And then… even more laughter.

Apparently, น้ำตาลปี๊บ is a traditional Thai syrupy palm sugar — so saying someone is "sweeter than palm sugar" is like calling them overly smooth or charming to the point of being suspicious. "มือไวเหมือนแมว"? That's someone who moves fast—usually in a flirty or mischievous way. And "ไอ้ฝรั่งนี่..."? That's me. The foreigner. The clueless-but-trying-his-best farang.

That night, I realized something important:

I could understand Thai… but I still didn't *get* Thai.

Let's change that.

In this chapter, we're going beyond grammar and vocabulary. You'll learn how native speakers use **sarcasm, irony, slang, and regional flavor** to communicate in ways that textbooks never teach you.

Because if you really want to think like a native, you don't just need the language.

You need the **humor,** the **attitude,** the **vibe.**

Let's dive in!

UNDERSTANDING THAI HUMOR, SARCASM, AND IRONY

When you first start learning Thai, you're taught polite greetings, useful travel phrases, and how to ask where the bathroom is.

What you're *not* taught?

That "เก่งจังเลยนะเรา" can mean the exact opposite of what it says.

Welcome to Thai Sarcasm

In English, sarcasm can be subtle. In Thai, it's often playful, ironic, and sometimes wrapped in a sweet smile that makes it even more confusing. If you don't know how to read the tone, you might walk away thinking someone just complimented you… when actually, you just got roasted with a grin.

Let's look at a few phrases:

- "เก่งจังเลยนะเรา"
  Literally: "Wow, you're so clever!"
  Meaning (with sarcasm): "Nice job screwing that up."
  Context: You just tripped while showing off your dance move.

- "สุดยอดจริง ๆ เลยนะ"
  Literally: "Truly amazing!"
  Meaning: "Seriously? That's what you did?"
  Context: You burned the rice for the third time.

- "เก๋ไก๋ไม่เบาเลยนะ"
  Literally: "How stylish!"
  Meaning: "What are you even wearing?"
  Context: You wore socks with sandals to a dinner date.

The sarcasm lives in the **tone**—drawn out, dry, and slightly mocking. Think eye-roll energy.

Humor Across Thailand: A Crash Course

Thai humor varies across regions, and understanding the local flavor can save you from those "wait… was that a joke?" moments.

Bangkok: Dry, playful, loaded with teasing

People from Bangkok love joking about your lateness, fashion choices, or your mispronunciation—with a smile that dares you to laugh with them.

Example:

- "มาก่อนเวลาอีกแล้วนะเรา"
  Translation: "You're early again, huh?"
  Actually means: "You're late. Again."

Isaan: Straightforward, earthy, often exaggerated

Isaan humor is lively, physical, and full of expressions that don't always translate. Expect laughter even before the punchline lands.

Example:

- "หน้ามนแต่จนกรอบ"
  Literal: "Cute face but broke as hell."
  Meaning: You're charming, but your wallet's empty.

Chiang Mai/Northern Thailand: Witty, subtle, sweetly sarcastic

Northern humor often uses a calm tone and poetic irony. You'll be gently roasted—and not realize it until a second later.

Example:

- "น่าฮักขนาดเลยเนาะ"
  Literal: "So cute, really."
- Meaning (depending on tone): Either sincere… or "You think that's cute?"

Misunderstandings That'll Get You Laughed At

Here's what happens when you don't *get* the joke:

You: "ขอบคุณมากที่ช่วยนะครับ!"
Thai person: "โอ๊ย ช่วยตลอดเลยล่ะ!" (deadpan)

You beam. "Wow! How kind!"

They walk away laughing because they absolutely did *not* help you—and they're teasing you for thanking them.

Or…

You respond seriously to **“มีแฟนกี่คนแล้วล่ะ?”** thinking it’s a real question. (It’s not. They’re making fun of your flirty vibe.)

In Thai, **a joke is often a test.** If you laugh, you’re in. If you miss it, you look stiff. But don’t worry—most learners fumble at first. And that awkward silence? Part of the learning curve.

Challenge: Decode the Humor

Step 1: Watch a Thai-language comedy sketch or stand-up clip (e.g., **Udom Taephanich, Note Udom,** or sitcoms like **Pen Tor or Bang Rak Soi 9**).

Step 2: Write down three phrases or lines that clearly *aren’t* meant to be taken literally.

Step 3: Reflect:

- What did they *actually* mean?
- How did tone, expression, or context change the meaning?

Final Thought

Sarcasm, irony, and humor are **fluency superpowers.** They show that you don’t just understand words—you understand *people*. So if someone says, **“อัจฉริยะจริง ๆ เลยเนอะ”** right after you spill coffee on yourself… smile, roll your eyes, and laugh. You’re one step closer to thinking like a native.

HOW TO DECODE SLANG AND FAST, REAL-WORLD CONVERSATIONS

You open your mouth to speak Thai. You're feeling good. Confident, even.

And then…

A native speaker hits you with:

"เฮ้ย ไงมึง เมื่อวานแม่งโคตรมันเลยว่ะ จริงป่ะ?"

Your brain: *Error. Rebooting.*

Suddenly, all those clean textbook sentences vanish like smoke. This isn't the Thai you studied. This is the **wild jungle of real-world conversation**—and you just got dropped into the middle of it without a map.

Welcome. Let's fix that.

Why Native Speech Feels Like a Blur

Let's be honest—textbooks lie.

They teach you things like:

- "คุณสบายดีไหมครับ?"
- "ฉันอยากกินข้าวผัดครับ"

But real people speak like:

- “เป็นไงบ้างอะ?”
- “อยากกินข้าวผัดว่ะ”

Native speakers contract words, skip particles, mash syllables together, and sprinkle in fillers like: “เอ่อ...”, “แบบว่า...”, “คือแบบ...”, “อะไรอย่างงี้อะ” constantly.

Throw in some slang, inside jokes, regional quirks, and... yeah. It's a verbal roller coaster.

Listening Hack: You Don't Need Every Word

Here's the truth: **Fluent listening is not about catching every word.** It's about catching **the meaning.**

In fact, native speakers often don't catch every word either. They rely on:

- **Tone**
- **Context**
- **Facial expressions**
- **Familiar phrase patterns**

So if you hear someone say:

- “แบบ...โคตรเกินอะแก”

Don't panic. You don't need to translate it word-for-word. You just need to sense:

- “That was totally over-the-top / extra.”

Useful Slang: Region by Region

Let's give you some **street cred.** These aren't phrases your textbook taught you, but they're **everywhere** in real conversations.

Bangkok:

- เฮ้ย – Hey / Dude
- แบบว่า... – Like… (filler)
- โคตรมัน – So much fun / Epic
- แม่ง – Damn / freaking (mildly vulgar, casual)
- จริงดิ? – Really?

Isaan (Northeastern Thailand):

- อิหลีบ่? – Really?
- หลายโพด – So much
- บ่เป็นหยัง – It's okay / No worries
- ม่วนแซ่บ – Fun and delicious
- เว้าเล่นเด้อ – Just kidding!

Northern Thailand (Chiang Mai):

- ฮู้าว – Yes (polite)
- ปุ๊กบ้าน – Go home
- กิ๋นข้าวล่ะกา? – Have you eaten yet?
- ขี้จุ๊ – Liar / Just teasing
- น่าฮักขนาด – So cute

Pro tip: Learn **10 slang phrases** per region and you'll blend in faster than a tuk-tuk in traffic.

What to Do When You Miss Something

You will blank out. That's normal. The key is how you **recover.**

Here's what to do:

1. **Don't freeze.** Keep eye contact. Nod. Stay present.
2. **Use survival phrases:**
   - “ขอโทษครับ พูดอีกทีได้ไหม?”
   - “แปลว่าอะไรเหรอ?”
   - “เมือกีไม่เข้าใจนิดนึง แต่พูดต่อเลยครับ”
3. **Echo what you did understand.** This shows you're engaged.
   - “อ๋อ เรื่องเมื่อวานใช่ไหมครับ เข้าใจๆ”
4. **Ask follow-up questions.** People love clarifying themselves.

Practice Challenge: Movie Mode

Step 1: Choose a fast-paced Thai series, movie, or comedy clip (YouTube, Netflix, or TikTok). Some great options:

- *Hormones: The Series*
- *Bangkok Traffic Love Story*
- *Ten Years Thailand*
- *Any skit by Note Udom or The Ska Film*

Step 2: Watch **without subtitles.**
Write down what you think is happening—even if it's rough.

Step 3: Rewatch with Thai subtitles.
What did you catch? What slang popped up? What did you miss?

Step 4: Try summarizing the scene in your own words—in Thai.

Final Thought

Understanding native Thai is like learning to dance in a nightclub—not a classroom. The lights are fast, the rhythm is wild, and everyone's got their own steps.

But the more you show up, the better you move.

So next time someone says, "โอ๊ย มันโคตรเว่อร์เลย!", don't panic. Smile. Nod. Say, "จริงเว่อร์!"

You'll be speaking like a native in no time.

ADAPTING TO REGIONAL DIALECTS WITHOUT LOSING YOUR MIND

You've finally got the confidence to speak Thai. You order your coffee, greet people on the street, even make small talk. You're feeling unstoppable.

Then you land in Chiang Mai.

The barista looks at you and says,
"จะเอาแกงฮังเลตวยกา?"

You pause.

Was that Thai? Was that a local spell? Did they just call me "กา"?

Welcome to the wonderfully chaotic world of **regional Thai dialects.**

One Language, Many Personalities

From the crisp Central Thai you learned from textbooks to the sing-song melodies of Northern Thai, to the bold bounce of Isaan, Thai isn't one single flavor—it's a buffet of voices, vibes, and vocab.

And just like Thai food... some are spicier than others.

But that's part of the fun.

Key Pronunciation Differences

Here's where your ears need a little flexibility:

Northern Thai (Lanna / Chiang Mai area):

- Soft, melodic tones
- Add polite particle "ก๊า" for women, "เน้อ" for both genders
- **Unique words like:** "ปิ๊กบ้าน" (go home), "กิ๋นข้าวแล้วกา?" (have you eaten?), "ขี้จุ๊" (liar)

Isaan (Northeastern Thailand):

- Lao-influenced
- Fun, bouncy rhythm
- Use of "เด้อ", "บ่", and verbs like "เว้า" (speak)
- **Common phrases:** "เป็นจั่งใด๋?" (how are you?), "หลายโพด" (very much)

Southern Thai:

- Faster tempo, clipped tones
- Often drops syllables or uses shortened forms
- Words can be hard for outsiders to catch without context (e.g. "เหนอ" instead of "ไหนอะ")

Vocabulary That Changes by Region

Same object. Totally different word. Here's proof:

English	Central Thai	Isaan	Northern Thai
Motorcycle	มอเตอร์ไซค์	จักรยานยนต์	รถเครื่อง
Sticky Rice	ข้าวเหนียว	ข้าวจี่ / ข้าวเหนียว	เข้าหนึบ
Grandma	ย่า / ยาย	แม่ใหญ่	ยาย / ป้าใหญ่
Shirt	เสื้อ	เสื้อ	เสิ่น
Delicious	อร่อย	แซ่บหลาย	ลำขนาด

And just when you think you've got it down…

You find out that **"ม่วน"** means **"fun"** in the North, but your Bangkok friend has no idea what you're talking about.

Stay calm. Breathe. You're not going crazy.

Should You Adapt?

Short answer: **You don't have to.**

If you're living in Ubon, **learn the local slang.** If your tutor is from Bangkok, **follow their lead.** But if you're just traveling or watching content from all over?

Stick to your base dialect (like Central Thai), but stay curious about others.

Your goal isn't to master every regional nuance—it's to **understand them** and adapt when necessary.

How Listening to Accents Makes You Smarter

At first, dialects may seem like a hurdle—but they're actually a **superpower in disguise.**

When you train your ear to recognize different accents:

- You become a faster listener.
- You stop relying on word-for-word understanding.
- You improve your comprehension across **all** forms of Thai.

It's like Muay Thai for your brain—tough at first, but it builds power.

Practice Exercise: Your 3-Dialect Drill

Step 1: Pick 3 short Thai clips, each from a different region. Options:

- **Central:** บุพเพสันนิวาส or Hormones
- **North:** Lanna YouTubers like "สาวเจียงใหม่"
- **Isaan:** TikTokers or sitcoms from GMM25 using Isaan dialogue

Step 2: Watch a 30–60 second scene from each, with no subtitles.

Step 3: Take notes:

- What words sounded different?
- Did you hear any slang?
- Could you catch the gist, even without understanding every word?

Step 4: Rewatch with Thai subtitles and compare.

You'll be surprised how much your brain picks up—even when it feels like chaos.

Final Takeaway

Dialects don't divide Thai. They **enrich** it.

They add texture, rhythm, and color to your fluency.

The more accents you embrace, the more Thai you'll sound—whether you're chatting in Chiang Mai, rapping in Rayong, or dancing at a night market in Korat.

So don't worry about sounding "too Isaan" or "too Bangkokian."

Be proud that you speak the language at all. Because most people never make it this far.

And you?

You're not just learning Thai anymore.

You're living it.

CONCLUSION:
Becoming the Thai You

At the beginning of this journey,

Thai may have felt like something outside of you—a system to master, a puzzle to solve.

But if you've made it this far, you've likely noticed something has shifted.

You're no longer just *learning* Thai.

You're *thinking* in it.

You're *feeling* in it.

You're beginning to **live** in it.

Language isn't just vocabulary and grammar—it's consciousness. It's the lens through which you see the world, the thread that links your inner voice to the people around you.

To think in Thai is not to replace English.

It's to **expand your awareness.**

To see two versions of reality.

To experience emotions in new textures.

To hold two worlds in one body.

You now carry that gift.

And the work doesn't stop here. In fact, the more fluent you become, the more invisible the effort will feel. One day, you'll say something in Thai… and not even realize it came out that way. You'll laugh in Thai. You'll dream in Thai. You'll *become* the Thai version of you.

That's when you'll realize—

This was never about memorizing words.
It was about **becoming more of yourself.**

Keep walking this path. Keep listening, feeling, making mistakes, laughing, connecting.

And if ever you feel lost, come home to the reason you started:
Not to master Thai… but to meet the version of you who speaks it.

I'll be cheering for you—wherever you are on your journey.

You may be holding this book in your hands, but the real transformation is happening in your mind, in your voice, and in your heart.

You've got this.

And if you ever want to connect, you'll find me at **www.seebbly.com** or on Instagram **@adriangruszka.**

Now go live your story—in Thai.

- *Adrian Gee*

Printed by Amazon Italia Logistica S.r.l.
Torrazza Piemonte (TO), Italy

74555697R00145